Cover Me!

To order additional copies of *Cover Me!*
by Filip Besim Zečević, call 1-800-765-6955.
Visit us at www.rhpa.org for information on
other Review and Herald products.

Filip Besim Zečević

REVIEW AND HERALD® PUBLISHING ASSOCIATION
HAGERSTOWN, MD 21740

Copyright © 2000 by
Review and Herald® Publishing Association
International copyright secured
All rights reserved

This book was originally published in the Croatian language. The original title was *Izgubljeno Nadjeno*. The book was translated by professor Damir Zugec.

The author assumes full responsibility for the accuracy of all facts and quotations as cited in this book.

Texts credited to NIV are from the *Holy Bible, New International Version.* Copyright © 1973, 1978, 1984, International Bible Society. Used by permission of Zondervan Bible Publishers.

This book was
Edited by Penny Estes Wheeler
Designed by Bill Kirstein
Desktop technician—Shirley M. Bolivar
Cover illustration by Marcus Mashburn
Typeset: 11/16 Palatino

PRINTED IN U.S.A.

04 03 02 01 00   5 4 3 2 1

R&H Cataloging Service
Zečević, Filip Besim
    Cover me!

    1. Zečević, Filip Besim   2. Bosnia and Hercegovina—Biography   I. Title

[B]

ISBN 0-8280-1566-X

DEDICATED
to
my beloved wife, Blanka,
and our son, Ruben.

ACKNOWLEDGMENTS

I would like to express my gratitude to those who have helped me with this book. I thank my wife, Blanka, who has patiently supported my work. I thank her for her help and understanding during the time of preparation and writing. I also thank Mrs. Djurdjica Garvanovic-Porobija, who, in addition to her duties as director of Marusevec High School, dedicated precious time to improve the literary quality. I also wish to thank Damir Zugec for translating this book into the English language, and my sister-in-law, Ivana Pino, and her husband, Jim, for their help.

In addition, I express my gratitude to many others who supported me with kind words and through their prayers. Thank you to Robert Folkenberg who told me that it was important that I share my story to the glory of God, and to Dr. Matak Dragutin who supported my writing.

Thank you, each one. May God bless you for the help you have given me.

CONTENTS

CHAPTER 1
Lost Life 15

CHAPTER 2
My First Baptism of Fire 21

CHAPTER 3
The House of Spirits and the Bunker of Life....27

CHAPTER 4
The Undestroyable 39

CHAPTER 5
Killed and Reborn 51

CHAPTER 6
Escape Into the Unknown 60

CHAPTER 7
The True Sign 69

CHAPTER 8
Stop the Earth, I'm Getting Off 81

CHAPTER 9
Back to Life...93

CHAPTER 10
God Leads 98

CHAPTER 11
A New Start 113

PREFACE

My dear friends, this book is written with you in mind. As I wrote my own story, I tried to bring an answer to the questions Why do the innocent suffer? or Why is it happening to me?

These questions pursue us all the time. Perhaps you too have frequently asked them of yourself. These questions are of eternal value and are among the most difficult to answer. More often than not, the answers elude us.

I would like to encourage you by saying that the answers may be very close to you; you will find them in a short time. I, myself, needed quite some time to find the answers—or rather recognize them. That is why I want you to recognize yourselves through this book and find encouragement in the fact that someone cares about you, although it is often not easy to see.

These pages will take you through the secret passages of my life; through moments when I felt utterly alone, friendless, and unprotected. On the other hand, you will meet my faithful Companion in good times and bad. The One who has never left me, not even when my life seemed to hang by a thread.

So come. Step with me into my life, and let this book become the first step of your own friendship with Him.

FOREWORD

If you hunger for sensations and, like the Athenians of old, ever yearn for something new (Acts 17); if you reach for a book to uncover another adventure, if curiosity led you to become acquainted with the war horrors in Bosnia and Herzegovina which shocked the whole world (and which you occasionally saw on a TV screen while having dinner, like some exotic and horrific dessert); if you want to learn about a man's life story and destiny; if you like miracles—these are still insufficient reasons for you to read this book.

But if you are ready to recognize the value of a personal encounter with God; if you are prepared to see God seeking for a man in the darkest and most hellish reality of this life; if you are willing to admit "Yes, He still acts today!" and thank Him, touched in your heart that God is good in word and deed toward the most humble; *then* you have the right qualifications to become a reader of this book. As readers have their right to choose books, so books have their right to choose readers. This book is looking exactly for that kind of reader—serious, refined, spiritual, and emotional—who knows the value of man and his heavenly Father, that Seeker for the lost ones.

What I find to be this book's exceptional treasure is the value of a human's response to God's search for her or him. The complete dedication that asks not for easy solutions, but rather searches for the true will of God. The author presents his life journey in a touching, almost childlike way. It is in this dedicated relationship between man and God that the central aesthetic value of this book is contained. This is the beauty of a true Christian experience.

The author, Filip Zečević, who is also the protagonist, wants this book to be inspirational, to make the reader think about God who is immensely active in our lives and who acts by His love.

—Djurdjica Garvanovic-Porobija, M. A.

CHAPTER 1

Lost Life

I'M ALONE, frighteningly alone, lying in a trench at the edge of a dry swamp. All is quiet. The frontline of the battlefield has been deathly silent for 24 hours. Not a crack of a twig, not a whisper of wind, not even the buzz of an insect or the bark of a distant dog. Time passes with agonizing slowness. The silence is unnerving

All I can see from my position in the bottom of the trench is high grass and reeds interlocked with fallen branches on all sides of me. To pass the endless hours, I punch small holes in the black earth by pounding in bullets with my fist. Then I fill the holes with gunpowder, light them with my cigarette lighter, and create my own mini fireworks display.

It's been a very long night. I guess I slept some. Now light filters through the grass and branches above me. I have no idea what this day may bring.

I glance at my improvised roof and feel annoyed at its poor construction. A child could have done better! It's so clumsily constructed I must twist my body like an acrobat just to look out. I stand up, knocking the roof with my helmet, and take a look around. Several haystacks are scattered across the field, their large beehive shape a perfect hiding place for the enemy. Morning seems an ideal time for them to attack.

Without a sound, I begin to crawl out of the trench to get a better view. Cautiously turning my head, I find myself looking point-blank into the dark beady eyes of a snake. It slithers slowly, silently toward me. Tension tingles through my hands and legs, knots my belly. Is it poisonous? Will it strike?

I can't advance toward the snake and I can't retreat back into the trench without taking my eyes away from it. My rifle is useless at such close range. Then I recall a scene from a movie; the actor grabbed a snake with his teeth! Do I dare attempt it? Could I move with such lightning speed? Soldiers are supposed to be brave, but inches away from possible death my courage has evaporated like morning mist.

I have no idea what makes me do it, but I quietly suck in my breath, then blow ever so gently through my pursed lips toward the snake. It seems surprised and lifts its head. I blow again. The snake freezes, then silently drops into the dry grass surrounding my trench and disappears.

My heart hammers in my chest as I lie down onto the dirt floor, my hand clutching my rifle. Should the snake reappear at the edge, that distance would allow me to blast him away.

Lying alone again with my thoughts, I ask myself why I'm here. Why in this trench, at this time? Why am I forced to lie here, waiting for an unseen enemy—a man like myself—to possibly creep on his belly from a haystack or across the field, a rifle in his hand. Is this life better than the one I knew a few months ago? Maybe it wasn't a great life but it was my life, and I had no fear.

I would wake up on a Sunday morning to the sound of birds singing as they fed in the orchard below my window. The sunshine streamed through my open window in narrow golden shafts and I'd stand and stretch, welcoming another lazy day. But those mornings now seem such a lifetime ago. What happened? Where did I go wrong?

I finished vocational school in Derventa, training as a home appliances repairman. After my required stint in the army, I got a job and started work. They're all suppose to be the right moves. After work I'd hang out downtown with my friends Igor, Buki, and Jasmin. We were close as brothers. We'd shoot pool and drink coffee in the cafés. The streets of Derventa were home for us; the town as familiar and comfortable as a well-worn shirt.

My father worked in a shoe factory, my mother stayed at home keeping house. Compared with many of the people of Derventa, we were pretty well off. We had a large house with garages and a garret. It had plenty of space for my friends to visit. My mother's cream cakes and strawberry and raspberry preserves from our abundant garden guaranteed that they would frequently stop by.

Then rumors began to circulate. The details were vague but we heard disturbing stories about a war that had started, or was expected to begin. Yet life in Derventa continued as it had for centuries. People went to work and came home and walked through the city as they always did. The town slanted down toward the river. On the other side of the river was a hill—called Grandmother's Hill—from which one could view the whole town as if on the palm of your hand. At the foot of the hill was a big army barracks stretching several miles, almost all the way to the river.

The town square drew us when we had free time. It was our favorite meeting place with numerous benches, and lit by street lights. No cars were allowed. Along the outer edge of the square were huge wild chestnut trees. We'd stroll to the fountain, sit on nearby benches, and just hang out. Across the street edging the square were the post office, the primary school, the library, a large Catholic church with twin towers high above the treetops, the town hall, and a mosque. These beautiful buildings seemed to look down on us with benevolent eyes.

As a boy, I often visited the mosque with my father, but as I grew up, I spent all my spare time with friends on the streets. The mosque still held a place in my heart, however, for when I had entered its doors to pray I had felt close to God. But as so often happens, when I became a teenager it wasn't the "in" place to be.

As the weeks passed, details of war intensified. Stories traveled fast. Frightening things. And though it seemed impossible, serious times were stalking ever closer to our secluded world where everyone seemed to like everyone else. I used to tell my father that in Derventa people didn't know how to quarrel. He'd just look at me with a knowing smile as if to say, you don't know us yet!

After my schooling was complete, I landed a job as an appliance repairman and found myself constantly on the road. As the weeks passed, I could not help but notice an increasing number of soldiers and military transports coming through our town. Soon it seemed that I saw them everywhere—in the town, in the surrounding woods, and in the smaller hamlets nearby. A few of the people of Derventa became military police. But my friends and I refused to be overly troubled, and still went regularly to concerts where songs of peace were popular.

Then suddenly Derventa was overrun with soldiers, military transports, and jeeps. They filled our peaceful streets right into the town square. They drove us off the streets so we could no longer relax in the cafés. I was scarcely able to see my girlfriend, Marina, for all workers now left their places of employment to get home before dark.

Within a week it was too dangerous to even walk through town. A few people had been murdered, and the *pop-pop-pop* of gunfire became the backdrop to our lives. Telephone lines were cut. We were enveloped in anarchy. We were living in the middle of a war about which we knew virtually nothing.

Our beautiful town had been divided into two sections. Soldiers in their barracks lived on one side, and the townspeople lived on the other. For safety's sake, we tried desperately to maintain a line of demarcation between the soldiers and ourselves. Many citizens acquired guns for self-protection, for sometimes soldiers opened fire without provocation. They destroyed our property, they attacked, they killed.

I lost all connection with Marina. She vanished, and I had no idea whether she was dead or alive. A few weeks before, such a situation would have been unthinkable. But now it was reality. My three best friends disappeared too. I felt an overwhelming sense of isolation, just as I now felt in this lonely trench. How I wished to see into the future. How I longed for hope!

CHAPTER 2

My First Baptism of Fire

She wore a bright red sweater. That's all I'll ever know of her.

The moment before she strode into view, I saw an enemy soldier, rifle at the ready, scanning the street around him. He moved his head slowly, deliberately, the gun barrel the indicator of the direction of his gaze. He wore camouflage clothing, and my instinct whispered that he was the enemy. I raised my rifle and took aim at him, but I wasn't a killer and I hesitated.

I'd never trained as a soldier. I had not been molded into a cog for a wheel in a killing machine, and I could not help but hesitate before pulling the trigger. I hated even the thought of killing someone. I'd shot bullets by the round without hesitation, but I'd never pointed my gun at anyone. I'd only shot "out there."

But my delay that day on a street of my hometown resulted in innocent death. In that moment a woman wearing a red sweater walked onto the street. The soldier pointed his rifle at her at point blank range and squeezed the trigger. She dropped instantly, silently to the ground. He walked away. He could have been shooting at a paper target for all the emotion he expressed. I felt weak and sick, then enraged.

As rumors of the war dragged on, edging ever closer to our small town, my mother and my sister, Suada, had left Derventa to stay with relatives in the south. For the moment they'd be safe there for fighting had not yet spread that far. Those of us who stayed in Derventa were drawn together, forced together, in a fight for survival.

We took good care of each other. We looked out for each other. At the beginning of the hostilities, nine of us on my street were just about old enough to volunteer for the army. Without any training we got rifles and did whatever we could to protect our town and the people who remained.

We served along the battle line that cut through the heart of our Derventa. For a while we didn't see much of the enemy. We felt the results of their attacks, but we never saw them face-to-face. For example, our small town hospital stood in the territory we controlled, and a constant stream of wounded flooded its doors and hallways. Naturally the hospital became a frequent target.

The morning I saw the murder of the woman in the red sweater, a neighbor took five of us downtown in his car to the demarcation line for our 12-hour shift. But before we got there, we became aware that the line had moved. The night had been filled with fighting. Commandos from the other side had spent the night ransacking our part of town. The bodies of the silent dead and groaning wounded lay in strange, grotesque positions in the streets. As we reconnoitered from a somewhat safe distance, we saw the raiders kidnapping people from where they'd hidden in their homes and basements. Some were pushed into vehicles, others were tied up and taken away. We wondered what their fate would be. One thing looked certain: the last remnants of our town's defenses were being crushed.

Our driver abruptly stopped the car at the edge of this battlefield. We spread out, standing alertly near street corners. My friend Robert and I walked into a concrete parking lot, protected by a low wall.

Moments later we saw a military transport making its way toward us carrying an antiaircraft gun. The crew fired wildly in all directions, not at any obvious targets, just demolishing everything in sight. As I watched, gaping holes were blasted into the walls of buildings as the transport slowly made its way down the street. Robert and I each had a rifle and two hand grenades—hardly a match for the heavily armored vehicle. We hit the ground as it drew abreast of us. Then, as it passed, we crept slowly in the direction from which it had come.

At first our utter innocence about warfare and a real reluctance to kill caused much loss of life. For example, that morning when we arrived in town and opened the car doors to get out, instantly the driver and another young man were wounded. Although injured himself, the driver rushed the boy to the hospital. We later learned that to get there they endured a hail of bullets, but they made it.

As we retreated from the transport, we realized that we'd walked into a part of town now controlled by our attackers. The parking lot where we'd hidden was blown up with dynamite a few moments after we left there, showering us with brick and glass fragments. Next the kindergarten down the street erupted in flames and quickly burned to the ground. It seemed unreal—gunfire and blood, explosions and fire. It was a nightmare, but it was reality.

I retreated another 100 yards or so to the left but found myself still in the fighting zone. I walked behind a high, thin wall surrounding a playground. But even small-calibre bullets were piercing the wall without difficulty. Robert and I felt painfully at risk and expected bullets to hit us at any moment. Before our frightened eyes the number of holes in the wall grew, and we became more and more exposed. Hunkered down to the ground, we decided to crawl slowly toward some trees in a nearby yard. I hadn't known until then that antiaircraft fire literally takes your breath away, even more so when it hits a building close to you. We experienced that as we crawled.

By now the gathering darkness began to drop its protecting mantle over us. The fighting continued, but we sensed that the firing had been designed to offer cover from the other side to the retreating commandos.

Lying under the trees with our faces to the ground, we became aware of a mist and presumed a smoke bomb had been dropped nearby. Then came more machine-gun fire, and flames blazed all around us, burning everything in their way. But the fire quickly burned out and then . . . we heard nothing but silence.

We had survived another today.

MY FIRST BAPTISM OF FIRE

We had not surrendered the town, and although our weapons and ammunition were very limited, we shot a few bullets every now and then just to show whoever was out there that we were alive, on duty, and still protecting our town.

This was not a game. It was not a movie. The ground was hard. Our bellies twisted with hunger and our hearts pounded with fear. And all through the streets, behind trees and walls, more young men crouched or lay, their fingers on their rifles. Not every one survived. Many young people were killed defending themselves and their town, and numerous civilians had been chased or dragged from their homes and shelters.

To dull the fear and pain we joked and fooled around.

The next day about 10 of us gathered behind an apartment building. A self-proclaimed commander, whom we knew to be a schizophrenic, decided to retrieve the wounded. On one hand, he was crazy enough to kill you if you disobeyed him; on the other hand, following his orders could also mean certain death. Some 20 yards away lay a man wounded in the legs. The commander sent a young boy to retrieve him—against all odds—across a sniper-covered area. Sure enough, snipers hit the boy before he got to the wounded man.

The commander asked for another volunteer to bring *that* boy back, saying that he would personally cover him. Another young boy agreed to go. This kid tidied up some personal belongings, picked up a piece of rope to drag the body, and left. Moments later he, too, lay on the pavement, dead in his blood.

I had watched a young man throw away his life because a fool told him to. How devastating! It was a turning point in my life, for on that fateful day I aged from a kid to a man.

By midnight we could see nothing, not a star, not even the slightest sliver of the moon. Such complete darkness covered the town that we had to communicate by whisper and touch. Here and there smouldering ashes stood out like vivid pictures against a dark velvet backdrop.

We decided to get as close as possible to the river Ukrina which flowed through the town at its lowest point. First we tried to walk along the street, but that proved impractical. Shells were scattered everywhere and as we hit them in the darkness they jingled and rolled, making a terrible noise that betrayed our position.

So Robert and I chose to make our way across the gardens of neighboring houses. We felt the way with our hands as we moved along. We feared ambush, land mines, and the presence of enemy soldiers and commandos.

Eventually we stumbled on a house. We were relieved, but a little frightened for we could not know who might be inside. However, it seemed to be secluded. Perhaps it would become our secret hiding place. We could never have dreamed what we were about to discover.

CHAPTER 3

The House of Spirits and the Bunker of Life

WE WERE desperate to find a safe place and thought this house might be it. In the thick darkness we could just make out the outline of a window. First we wondered if anybody had found this place before us, and if so, were they friend or foe. Standing motionless, hardly breathing, we strained to hear the slightest sound of human life. But we heard nothing. After a time we felt adventuresome enough to attempt to raise the window. Feeling around the perimeter of the window frame, we learned that its glass was missing. We reached inside, found its lock, opened it, then gently lifted the window. Still no sound, still no evidence of life. I climbed on Robert's shoulders and silently, carefully eased myself through the window and onto the floor. Robert followed.

We were blind in the darkness. Feeling around with his hands, Robert identified a chair. We placed it under the window to use as a stool in case we needed to make a hurried exit. Then we continued to explore the first room. We felt another chair, and another, and another. The room seemed to be filled with chairs. Why would anyone need so many chairs? we wondered. After a time we felt secure enough to light a cigarette lighter and use it to see to explore.

We concluded that we had climbed into what must have been the largest room in the house. Exploring by the lighter's faint flame, we found more and more chairs, but not one bed, closet, television set, or kitchen stove. We wondered if this house could possibly be a comfortable building in which to live and hide.

As we crept on, we suddenly felt chilled air on our faces. We were outside again! Well, not quite, but it seemed that half the house had been blown away. Perhaps all the living quarters had been demolished, leaving just the Great Room behind. On one side of the opening we noticed a curtain hanging by a corner. When morning dawned we fastened the other corner on an exposed nail to create a makeshift screen against the outside world. We moved two chairs from behind us and took our box office seats, ready to view the backyard—or maybe the front—when the first rays of sun began to filter through the trees. As we waited, we could hear the murmur of the river from a distance, but no other sound competed for attention. A tomb could not have been more silent.

Exhaustion overtook us as we began to relax in our newly found place of security. We were so tired that we had no strength even to talk. We were desperate for sleep, but we dared not sleep until we knew we were safe. I placed the muzzle of my rifle under my jaw to prod me should my head fall forward in sleep. But in vain. Just before the dawn, drowsiness overcame me, and despite the muzzle, I fell asleep.

I awoke in the early dawn to the refreshing touch of early morning mist on my face. Looking straight ahead I was startled to see a man walking toward me through the grass. As I watched, he jumped the fence. I lifted my rifle, then stood and yelled, "Halt!" He froze. I released the safety catch as noisily as possible, hoping he would hear. "Hands up, or I'll kill you!" I shouted. He put his hands behind his neck.

I didn't know what to do next. In the past few days the importance of caution and self-protection had been burned into my consciousness. Should I kill him and take myself out of danger? If he happened to be a trained commando, he might have a hand grenade hidden behind his back and on an impulse might throw it at me. I had to be cautious for self-protection. "Put your hands in the air!" I called. He obeyed. I had no idea what to do next.

I could not afford to make a mistake. If I misjudged the situation, I could be the one that ended up dead. My heart throbbed in my temples. I fought to keep my hands from trembling. After what seemed a very long time, I ordered, "Get out onto the street!" He passed by me very slowly, his hands still held above his head.

"Don't do it, brother," he said as he drew abreast of me. "By your children, don't kill me, please."

"Stop where you are!" I commanded, "and don't turn around!"

"Oh, my mother," I heard him exclaim.

A small group of my friends were coming toward us. As they came closer they looked surprised to see me guarding a prisoner. I handed the poor fellow over to them and went back to my self-appointed guard post at the back of the house.

In the emerging daylight, life seemed more relaxed. And in the early light of day we discovered more about the building we'd stumbled upon the previous night. The reason for all those chairs became obvious; the reason for no beds and cupboards; the reason for no kitchen. We had stumbled on a church, a bombed-out red brick church.

Over the next few days we explored every corner of the old church. We tried to play the church organ, but it refused to yield its heavenly melodies to a bunch of mocking soldiers. The greatest mystery for us lay in three rows of numerals on the wall. We were mystified as to what such numbers could mean in a church. There were nine numbers, in three rows of three. I remember them to this day: 3 6 5, 1 7 5, 2 5 0. We just couldn't figure it out.

"Perhaps it's a crossword puzzle," Robert suggested.

"Come on, when have you ever seen a crossword puzzle in a church?" I asked.

"Maybe it's a mathematics problem," Edin offered.

So we added them up every possible way, vertically, horizontally, and diagonally. But those numbers never revealed their secret to our group of mocking soldiers. And there was no way we could have guessed the simple solution: that these mysterious numbers told the congregation what hymns to sing on the last Sabbath they met together.

Outside the building stood a crumbling sign but the name of the church could still be read: Christian Adventist

Church. We were a bunch of Muslims, and we had no idea what this Christian church could be about.

As the days passed, we tried to make ourselves comfortable. We used the chairs to sleep on. We arranged them in rows, and with stolen blankets we made ourselves some narrow, but relatively comfortable, beds.

Then our small group began a systematic search of the area looking for signs of life, but we found none. Not a civilian could be seen. The wounded and the dead had been cleared off the streets, yet the evidences of their efforts and the price they paid in blood were everywhere.

In the past few hours a new front line had been established as we'd been driven back. We had to learn which roads were safe and which were dangerous, which buildings were safe and which were dangerous. Each day Robert and I returned to our building and tried to make ourselves comfortable. Two friends joined us there, Edin and Emin.

Day after day we watched a big, tall gypsy stride down that street, and every single time he had more and thicker golden chains and rings. He always had a video recorder under his arm, wrapped in a blanket. We realized that all day long he'd snoop around for new treasures. He even started using a supermarket cart to carry his booty around, and often he'd stop by and boast about his latest finds.

We had one cooked meal a day. I would get our tea and sausages while Robert was in charge of soup. I'd return with the sausages hanging on one arm in long coils, almost dragging on the ground. With the other arm I cradled a container of tea. One day as we were exchanging our habitual jokes—"Let's not run like mice, we're carrying food." "We're not such unlucky devils as to be attacked on such a mission."—we suddenly heard an outburst of fire in our direction. We ran with our food, laughing at ourselves. We must have looked like regular clowns. We made fun of everything. I suppose that was our way to let off steam.

Many people—civilians and soldiers—were killed by snipers in just this way. What did it matter? Just one less person in the world. Sometimes one could cross the road 10 times in a row and nobody would even open fire. Then just one shot would be fired, and the bullet would hit its mark. Some poor folks were killed just a step or two before reaching their shelter, in the last moments before reaching safety when they'd slowed from running to walking. Death was a normal everyday occurrence.

Two blocks uphill from our post was a broad street that had to be crossed in order to get to the Civic Center where one of the other posts was located. Many people ran across that stretch every single day. Snipers had it in clear view, and they were quite active. On one side was the Civic Center and a guarding post; on the other side a house painted blue with a single door in its front. No windows. We'd pause at the house and prepare to run for it. We installed a machine-gun nest at a corner of the house to cover the admittance from the nearby bridge.

Frankly, it was more of a ploy than a real danger to the enemy. The clearance stretched for some 10 or 15 yards.

THE HOUSE OF SPIRITS

One day a guy who was taking food to his post was surprised by an outburst of machine-gun fire. The bullets struck the pavement right in front of him. He was forced to withdraw, so he jumped behind a thick linden tree. He spent hours there, hidden behind the tree. The sniper played a game of nerves with him, hour after hour blasting away pieces of bark from either side of the tree. Eventually, the man got out of that tight corner alive, by using an old trick—falling to the ground as if mortally wounded.

The good thing about that post was that the old house provided a secure shelter within its three-foot thick walls. Only its entrance was dangerous. A candy store had used the building as a warehouse, so we found an almost endless supply of soft drinks stacked there for us to enjoy. There were empty bottles scattered around all over the place. We used to fool around with the guys across the road at the blue-colored house. We'd spin bottle caps at them or shoot tracer bullets above their heads for fun. The tracer bullets usually hit the roof of the blue house. These were not real slugs with killing power. We'd usually find them later, sometimes using them for tracing, sometimes just for fun. They flew wildly, zigzagging in their way. Sometimes in the night we could see a bullet fly straight for a 100 yards or so, then suddenly turn aside or upward, spiraling around in its brilliant flight.

Once one of these hit some old books in the attic. My school friend Amir was over there and I warned him that his roof was on fire. He just sat, leaning back against the wall, smiling, taking it for a joke. When I ran to the cellar to get a fire extinguisher he finally took me seriously and looked up. Smoke was billowing out through the roof tiles. I ran across the street and we climbed up to the attic together. Tons of scrap paper and books were stored up there. Smoke was everywhere. We put on our masks, rushed in with fire extinguishers in our hands, and just barely managed to put the fire out. Then we went out, sat leaning against the wall, and smoked. We spent the rest of that day together. There were occasional outbursts of enemy fire but it didn't feel like another general attack any time soon. The enemy was just letting us know they were there, to which we'd reply in the same way.

Later that same day something extremely odd happened to me. It was such a powerful experience that even to this very moment I shiver every time I remember it. A few shells hit the ground rather close to where we were, so we started to muse whether to stay there or leave to someplace safer. In no time at all, we heard another batch of shells whizzing through the air. Amir rushed through the front door into the house, but I was caught halfway between the wall and the street.

Something outside myself forced me to freeze in a running position for a few seconds, then three shells exploded two or three yards away. I stared at the spot where they'd hit, and considered myself dead. The detonation shook me up badly. The world was hidden by dust and smoke. Pieces of shrapnel cut through some flowers, roses I think. Time stood still. I felt as though I were living through a slow-motion movie and couldn't tell if I was still alive or not. I was showered by pieces of mortar torn off the facade of the building, and yet I couldn't feel anything. I couldn't tell if I still had my arms or legs. I still had my sense of sight; that was all I could be sure of. No pain at all.

In a state of shock, I ran into the house after Amir and we took shelter under a staircase, waiting for that bout of shelling to cease. I couldn't believe that I hadn't been wounded. But I examined my body and there was no blood. Later we went out and found the area devastated, the entire wall was pockmarked by pieces of shrapnel. Only one part of the wall, the size of a door, was intact. It was exactly where I'd been standing. I wasn't even scratched!

For the rest of the day I went around like a ghost, aimlessly shuffling my feet, wondering if I were dead or alive. What had stopped me in mid stride? I knew that logically I should have been killed. However, the few square feet of standing wall proved that I was still alive. I had a strange feeling in my stomach, as if it was filled with helium, as if I were hollow.

But life-and-death events of war happen so quickly that you hardly react to one before something else occurs. Every event in war has just a short span of providing one with excitement, so this one, too, lost much of its impact by nightfall. The only thing that mattered was living for today. Sometimes we toyed with our lives, but there were moments when we took utmost care to keep our heads safely upon our shoulders. But sometimes we wondered what was the point of still living when we could be killed at any moment.

"Why should a child get killed? What has it done wrong?" Robert mused. "If I get killed, well, here I am on the front line, so that makes sense. But why an innocent baby? What is God doing? Why, Oh God, why?"

We felt corruption in every single thing around us—sudden death, the lowliness of morality and human behavior, the nastiness of life. Streets were covered by rotting spills of food thrown out of refrigerators and freezers. Mounds of rotting garbage were scattered along the street and we held our breath against the stench as we ran past them.

We had another friend with us—Srecko, a boy of some 17 or 18 years of age. He was a good soldier and a better friend. But he'd often become gloomy, so one day I asked what was the matter.

He told me. Just before the whole mess started he'd spent some time with his father, and then they'd parted. Srecko was defending his town and his buddies, while his father was the captain of a tank unit on the other side, blasting the town from a position not far off. They parted as people with different goals. Yet they still loved each other as father and son. What a weird brew, this mixture of good and evil, happiness and unhappiness, joy and sorrow, victory and defeat. The overall feeling was one of emptiness. All values had been lost. If only there'd been a way out of that misery! But there wasn't. We were trapped. We hadn't asked to be separated from our homes and families. We hadn't asked to live from heartbeat to heartbeat. We had no choice. All we could do was fight for our lives, or die.

It was puzzling. We couldn't figure out what people from other towns were doing in our town. We found some stuff left behind by a blaster whose job had been to blow up some apartments—a pile of dynamite, a bag full of blasting equipment, and all of his papers. We just couldn't figure it out. We read one of the documents: Person this and this, militarily ranked as . . . , is to be paid 100 Deutschmark for each day spent in combat, in his endeavor to liberate . . .

What was that? What did it mean? Had people come to our town from Austria, Slovenia—wherever—to fight for 100 Deutschmark a day? Why? On this man's body was his passport, complete with visas and passes. It was insane. Did he need money that badly? He lost his life for 100 Deutschmark.

A more immediate question, however, was why did *I* keep losing my friends, my town, and my future? Possibly, my own life. We were haunted by that question, "Why," but there was no answer.

The man I'd taken prisoner was a civilian after all. We found that out the following day. He'd been forced out of his apartment as a hostage, and was taken across the river to work. After he saw people killed in cold blood he feared for his own life and decided to try to escape. Escape would greatly improve his chances of survival. He made a simple plan with another man in his group, and they ran away in opposing directions. He spent one whole day and night in the sewers. He was beaten up, but could walk. The other man was seriously wounded, still hiding in some other hole. Our guys organized a search party and managed to find the other one. These two men proved to be valuable eyewitnesses as they knew about a large amount of ammo. It had been left behind by some commandos as its bulk and weight had slowed them down. There was a big box of grenades, and some rocket launchers as well.

Our primary goal was to survive, against all odds. In no circumstances was one to surrender. We attended the funeral of a former schoolmate, Tony Krola. We honored him by firing a round into the air. He was buried in something hardly larger than a shoebox as he'd been burned up after being crushed between two cars. Only his tennis shoes and his socks remained intact. He died senselessly.

When demarcation lines disappeared, Tony had started to play the fantasy role of Rambo. He rushed into one dangerous situation after another, until the fateful day he was wounded and set on fire. For days after the funeral his father kept whispering, "That's not my Tony. He's still alive somewhere."

Sadly, everybody else knew it had been Tony, as no one else wore tennis shoes like his. Anyway, he never showed up again. Almost every single day someone lost a loved one, a neighbor, some relatives, one's very sanity and will to live. But life just went by.

CHAPTER 4

The Undestroyable

I'M ON guard duty in our secret "church in the woods." I fill the tedious hours sitting on a chair behind a chest of drawers topped with bookshelves filled with books. Glass doors once protected the books, which I presume are valuable, but the glass now lies shattered on the floor. One forlorn, torn curtain moves languidly with each gentle stir of wind.

Outside the day is bright and sunny. It's noon and I haven't heard a shot since yesterday. It seems like a good time to steal some rest. The chest of drawers and books will be my protection.

I might as well read to put myself to sleep, I think, looking at the books. *Nothing's going to happen at noonday.* I pick up a thin volume. It's been a long time since I've read a book, so I choose the slimmest spine I can find in order to ease my way back into the gentle art of reading. I begin at page one but within seconds find my thoughts wandering.

If she'd waited just 20 seconds, she wouldn't be in the hospital now . . .

It's all my fault . . . No, it isn't. . . . How could I have known that my late return home last night would have such terrible consequences for my mother?

The disastrous sequence of events began when we were forced to move to another battlefront outside our town. We were ferried there by truck, covering ourselves with a tarpaulin while we traveled. Each trip added a few more bullet holes to the tarpaulin.

Then on one occasion when Emin and I were out on patrol, we found a car in pretty good condition and hot-wired it. For the next few days, five of us from the same neighborhood drove home in it. We were far less conspicuous in this car than in a truck with a yellow tarp, and even more important, we were independent. When that old car turned into our street, we heard cheers from all our friends.

Then one day my friends drove home without me. I stayed on the front line a few extra minutes to help some other soldiers, telling my buddies that I'd come home shortly in the truck.

My mother had gone to stay with relatives at the beginning of the war, but she'd returned home the day before. There was no reason to stay any longer. All her relatives had been taken prisoner, along with everybody else in their village. My sister, Suada, had already moved to another place where she lived alone. Until yesterday I'd heard no news of her for some time. Suada also came home hoping our unit would return safe and sound.

During yesterday's gunfire and shelling, I headed for the truck to go home. Bullets whizzed about us as we ran for cover. My group had left by car about 10 minutes earlier. Then two tank grenades flew over us, moving ominously in the direction of our town. I knew they were targeted at the hospital.

We finally made it home, and when I jumped off the truck at the corner of my street I saw a huge crater in the middle of our road. Stones and dirt from the explosion were scattered over some 50 yards of pavement. I learned from the neighbors that my mother had been wounded, so I ran to the hospital.

"She's alive and we're stitching her up. You can't go in yet," a nurse told me. A few minutes later they wheeled Mother into the corridor and we hugged.

"My son, you're alive!" she greeted me painfully.

"Yes, Mom, I'm here, and I'm alive."

When I didn't arrive with my group in the auto, as I'd done for several days, she grew impatient and concerned. My friends assured her that I'd be fine. I'd only stayed to help some soldiers, and I'd arrive soon. Still her mother's heart worried, and she waited in our garden near the garage where she could take shelter if more shells came overhead. From that vantage point, she could see any vehicle turning into our L-shaped street.

My mother maintained an impeccable garden. Her eyes were constantly on the lookout for weeds. Standing by the garage, she saw a weed and told herself, *I'll pull it out, then come back here and he'll be here soon.* But away from the shelter of the garage, standing in her beautiful garden, she'd been hit by a shell fragment. It was the same shell I had heard overhead; the same shell that had jolted me with a premonition of danger. The fragment hit her in the back, drove into her chest, and stopped neatly wedged between her spine and heart. Mother had to stay in the hospital. The doctors in the little field hospital could not extract the fragment.

Over and over again my mind replayed the events of that afternoon, feeling sad and worried and guilty, wondering how I might have changed the course of events. But you can't turn back the clock.

When we were back in the village from the front line we engaged in a lot of horsing around. We'd do almost anything to distract ourselves from the terrifying scenes of the front lines. But even the town could be a dangerous place.

On one occasion, five of us heard the faint sound of firing grenades so we headed for safety in the nearest building, a town square church. There we waited to see where the grenades would land. One fell close by; we could tell by the powerful detonation; then another, and another.

Suddenly shells were exploding all around the church. They weren't falling one at a time, but several at a time. We hit the floor between the pews, flanking each other. Shell fragments tore at the church facade, and mortar fell from the ceiling. The front window overlooking the street rattled, and piece by piece the glass panes shattered and fell to the floor.

We were trying to act nonchalantly, and poked fun at the shelling while Robert counted the exploding grenades. Closer and closer they came to where we lay. The more they fell, the quieter we became, until finally we lay between the pews, scared and silent. All except for Robert. He measured the moments with the tally of mortars between blasts: "...25...26...27..." The roof of the church was made of wood. It wouldn't protect us from the shelling, and we knew that if we took a direct hit we'd all be dead. With the window now demolished the sound of approaching grenades grew even louder. The flower beds and lawn in the church yard were torn apart. Ultimately even Robert lay as silent as a cadaver, and only the exploding grenades spoke.

Quietly, self-consciously, I found myself silently mouthing the words of a prayer: "God, if there is a God, save me. Stop this horror." I would not be surprised that each of us lying on the floor that day were saying a similar prayer, calling out to a God they hardly knew, but hoping, looking for a miracle—survival. And when it was over I had to admit that in a remarkable way the prayer seemed to have been answered. The grenades landed in a circle around the church; we saw the little craters pockmarking the ground and the street on all sides. But not one grenade hit the church directly. Somehow, God—if there is a God, we reasoned—had protected His own house.

When all was quiet, we got up from the littered floor and left the church. We were silent, speechless, grateful.

Days passed. Often I found myself thinking about miracles. Was it possible that there is a God, and that He had somehow kept five young unbelieving guys alive? The war had brought devastation to me, my family, our town, my friends. Someone had to take the blame for all this. I questioned the whole existential thing, and the question of evil. Why were both the good and the bad dying in this war? *If* there was a God, why did He allow it? What kind of God could He be? Why was my mother injured? What kept her from being killed?

I recalled the inscription at the front of the church: "Come unto me . . . Jesus." What an empty invitation. What good did Jesus do for my relatives taken prisoner from their homes by the enemy? What good did Jesus do for those of us caught in this terrible war?

On several other occasions we took shelter in the same town square church. And while I felt some physical protection, mentally it made me angry. Every time I jumped through the window to relative safety I'd see that phrase, the invitation beginning with the word "Come." Anger filled me at such a stupid sentiment. Once I stood there, my finger on the trigger of my machine gun, almost overcome with the urge to blast the words into oblivion. But for some odd reason I didn't pull the trigger.

A short time later, while on guard duty in our "church in the woods," I sat reading a magazine. Through a strategically positioned mirror, I could see out of the building and across the landscape in front of us. That view helped protect us from sniper fire.

A few minutes later Robert came by and said, "I'm going to that house over there to see if I can find something to eat or drink. Cover me just in case."

"OK," I replied, continuing to read, but glancing in the mirror to assure myself all was clear. Then I stood up to take a closer look. "You can't be too confident in situations like this," I told myself. I looked out the window, checked the surrounding buildings, saw nothing suspicious, and sat down again to read. But feeling a little uneasy, a few minutes later I got up to take another look. As I approached the window, someone yelled "Besim!"

I stepped back and looked around, but could see no one. In that moment I heard gunfire, a few rounds one after another. Glancing toward the window, I realized that bullets were whizzing through the window, *the spot where I would have been standing*! When I'd first heard the gunfire, I supposed Robert must have been shooting from the front door. Then I realized a sniper had been shooting at me, and someone had covered me.

I walked back into the church and asked, "Who called me?" Some of the guys were lying down. Others were playing cards. One of them yelled at me for shooting from my post, because that increases the chances of being shelled. You don't shoot from the place where you're hiding if you can help it. Then the truth sank in—none of them had called me! I asked about Robert, and they said he'd left the building through a window. I knew he'd been shooting at the sniper.

But someone had called me. I'd heard a shout: "Besim!" *Who had done it? Who had called me by name?*

A few days later, taking refuge in the old church in the woods, the same questions returned to haunt me. *Why had my life been spared? Why had others lost their lives? Why had my mother become a victim of a shell frag-*

ment? I felt spared, but doomed as well.

Sitting in the church, I tugged at one of the neatly arranged copies of the Bible that stood in the bookshelves without glass protection. I tried to pick up one after the other, but they would not come out. Then I forced a copy from the shelf and realized the volumes had been bound together by the bullets they had absorbed! The copy I held in my hands was in fairly good condition, so I opened the first page and started reading about the creation of the world. But I immediately felt a sense of annoyance and thought to myself, *What's the big deal about all this? Everyone knows this stuff.* I struggled on through three chapters and then paused to think about what I had read. It all seemed so confusing. *What's God doing placing a curse on Eve and the serpent?* I wondered. It didn't make any sense to me.

I'd picked up another book, *The Cosmic Conflict*, and opened it in the middle, reading something about demons and fallen angels. I'd never read anything like that before. It was interesting enough, but my confusion was so deep that I tossed the book aside.

As days drifted by in a blur of battles, bullets, and blood, it seemed obvious that conditions were deteriorating. Every day now, the enemy deliberately set two or three houses on fire. Our post had deteriorated, but it didn't matter. We'd lost all desire for comforts; we just didn't care. We didn't even go home for several days at a time. Countless bullet holes marked the walls of the church; in fact the walls were beginning to look like a sieve. And one day while walking past the church I noticed that the sign outside had been almost completely destroyed. *Good riddance,* I thought to myself. Everything seemed to be bullet-riddled, burned, or deserted. It demoralized us all.

The next day a house across the street from the church had been set on fire, along with a 60-foot-long pile of chopped firewood. It took a long time to burn out and the fire blazed so violently it sent glowing embers into the sky day and night like a giant open stove.

The town square church, a bastion of stateliness and propriety, had been taken over by some secular townsfolk. Someone brought in a stereo and speakers and blasted music while kids ate, and drank, and danced. Edin and the rest of us were forced to go to the basement in a nearby house to catch some rest.

That same afternoon, while Edin slept, the house caught on fire from igniting bullets. We watched the smoke and blaze for a short time until we remembered that Edin had gone there to rest! I ran to the house and tried to get into the basement. I could hear burning rafters falling down, and roof tiles after them. I beat on the door trying to wake Edin. The basement had pretty much filled with smoke by this time, and he would soon suffocate if we didn't get him out. After what seemed an eternity, Edin awoke, and we all ran from the house in confusion, gunfire still around, our entire world going up in smoke. For a while Edin didn't know whether he was living or dreaming.

That day we were forced to leave the town. Hastily packing our few belongings into a car, we jumped in and began to roll out. As we drove down the street one of the guys yelled, "Hold on, where's Edin?" We stopped, got out of the car, and went back to the town square church. Music still blared through the open window frame, the sounds of battle were still in the background. We spotted Edin sitting at a carefully positioned mirror holding his rifle in one hand and a bottle of brandy in the other.

"Dino, let's go!" we yelled to him.

He glanced up. "We're leaving?" he asked calmly. "Where are we going? May as well die here as any place else."

"We know that," I told him. "No one has anywhere to go, but we may as well stick together." The only direction our families could have gone would have been Bosanski Brod. Edin got the message and decided we probably should stick together. Thus we set off, leaving behind Derventa, the town we loved, the home town of our entire childhood and youth.

Ten miles up the road we came to a roadblock. All cars had been stopped, and crowds of people were everywhere. They blanketed the road and the fields beside the road. We couldn't move. We waited for a while until we came to the realization that political foul play lay behind all this. The military police were sending people back. They wouldn't let anyone through. We turned the car around and headed back to Derventa. A dozen or so cars followed us.

By the time we arrived back in town, we learned that it had been deserted for about six hours. We had been the last ones to leave, and we were the first to return. We saw just one other car at the entrance road and in it were some of our friends from the front line, Smajo, Alem, Ado, and Samir. The 10 of us decided we would defend the town! We spread out and sent off a volley of bullets from odd places in short bursts throughout the night. In the morning we withdrew to an office building.

For the next few days we acted as an efficient small fighting unit. But the enemy attacks continued and ultimately we were forced to leave a second time. On foot we followed a middle-aged man we considered the leader of our self-formed unit. The journey proved to be sheer terror. We had no idea where we were. For safety we walked by night, but even in the moonlight we could see charred ruins everywhere. One moment we walked on soft ground that absorbed the sound of our footsteps, the next moment we clomped on hard ground though we tried to step as quietly as possible. After about an hour, we came to the road where cars were waiting for us.

The next morning we found another group that had been stopped at the same roadblock. We all took cover in the back yard of a house for a few hours. We all wanted to reach Bosanski Brod. Later that day we agreed we should try again, but as soon as we started, planes appeared and began to strafe us. One bomb fell in a yard we'd just left. The planes forced everybody in the area to take refuge. We didn't, so when we got to the roadblock we drove straight through to Bosanski Brod unchallenged.

But we were not welcomed in Bosanski Brod. Up to this time Bosanski Brod had been in the rear of the battle;

our arrival put the town at the front line. Until now the war had not touched the town very much. Life had continued with little change. Unlike Derventa, the shops and cafés were open, and electricity and running water were still available. But best of all I found my parents! They'd taken shelter in the house of a woman who, years before, had heard of my mother from some distant relatives. The main thing she remembered about my mother was her knitting skills. That fact made her welcome in the house, and several other refugees from our street in Derventa were admitted also.

Being with my family again forced on us the realization that we needed to keep the enemy as far away from this town as possible. With that objective in mind we arranged shifts and methodically traveled everyday as far as we could down the road to Derventa. In this way we did all in our power to keep our friends and family alive.

CHAPTER 5

Killed and Reborn

It TOOK time to get used to fighting at a different front line. It meant we had to cope with new dangers, to anticipate surprises, and to learn to fight in the rain. We were soaked to the skin day and night.

Our group had divided into two alternating patrols, each lasting two or three days. We were housed near the river on the outskirts of a demolished part of town. We were driven to the front line, some 10 miles away, by bus or truck. The road ran through a narrow ravine for a few miles, which made us vulnerable to attack. We didn't have enough men to defend the road, so at any moment a shell or a rocket could hit us. We felt as if we were riding on a bus of death each time we drove that stretch. And if the bus itself was not an obvious enough target, it churned up a great cloud of dust from the dirt road, practically shouting to the enemy that a new patrol had headed out for duty.

This front line was established on the edge of a dried-out marsh, as I described in Chapter 1. Five-foot reeds grew in front of us providing important cover, but the trench I lay in had been crudely constructed. Another trench had been dug some seven feet to our left. We spent entire days in these ditches. Three of us hid in this particular trench—Alen and Smajo, who had been friends for a long time before the war, and myself. To pass the time we joked around. And every day we made our way back some 500 yards to collect food and water.

On one occasion Smajo stayed in the trench while Alen and I went for supplies. It was a beautiful day to be away from the front line and I was enjoying it. A number of other soldiers from similar positions joined us in the spacious yard of the house where we'd collect more food and draw water from a well. The lawn was well cared for, as lovely as the house. Ambulance drivers, soldiers, and the men who brought the food to the field all mingled together sharing stories and telling jokes. I filled our bottles with water, got the rations, then sat down under a gazebo overgrown with grapevines to eat lunch. My friends Emin and Edin were already seated at a table so I joined them, sitting on a small stool. I had a carton of milk, and placed it upright in the grass beside my stool. Several doctors and drivers sat on the front doorsteps of the house eating their lunch. We'd all leave to return to our positions in the field at about the same time.

Suddenly we were startled by the sound of gunfire, and a heartbeat later several bullets whizzed around us. While trying to determine the source of the gunfire, a strange thought zipped through my mind: *Put the milk on the table out of harms way.*

Instantly, without conscious thought, I followed the instinct. I bent down, picked up the milk and lifted it onto the table. Then, looking up, I spotted the gunfire coming from one of the drivers that had been sitting on the top stair. As he stood up after eating his lunch, he'd unintentionally pulled the trigger of his submachine gun. Instantly, bullets sprayed across the yard. I saw one bullet hit the leg of a driver, the shooter's own brother. Next the gun swung around toward some other men, and then I saw it directed at us.

Automatically, I reached into my trouser pocket for a bandage. A lot of blood could flow as the result of an instant of clumsiness. Edin and Emin jumped from their stools and looked directly at me. The drivers had been sitting to my left, and after another quick check in their direction I turned my head to the right to check on Alen. He wasn't there. Then I spotted a form by my side, draped over the stool where I'd been seated just seconds before. Edin and Emin saw it too. It was Alen.

"Alen!" I yelled. He gave no response. I grabbed his shoulder and lifted his head from the stool on which he had fallen. I'd never seen him in such a strange position, even while bent over in prayer in the mosque. I couldn't quite grasp the situation. "Alen," I called again, pulling him up straighter. But even as I tried to lift the dead weight of his body his hands remained on the stool. His face was pale, but I couldn't see any wounds. A tiny trickle of blood ran from his nose. Looking closer, I saw a small wound in his forehead.

"Alen!" I shouted, as if raising my voice would make him hear. But he still gave no response. Emin pressed a handful of bandages to his forehead and with Edin's help, carried him to a nearby car. All around us others had quickly focused their attention on the wounded, carrying them to cars which sped off to the hospital. It was hard to believe that so much damage could happen in such a brief time.

There was nothing else to do, so a short time later I returned to our trench, alone. I felt devastated. The 500 yards seemed to take forever as I lifted one heavy foot, then the other. I had no idea how I'd tell Smajo what had happened to his friend. But waiting there by himself, he'd heard the shots and was anxious to know the situation. And so, while my shaking hands kept busy stacking the food and milk in the trench, I told him everything. I described our peaceful lunch, the sudden spray of bullets, and Alen's still, heavy body carried to a car.

Smajo's mouth contorted with grief. He looked grotesque, but if I hadn't known the truth, I could have thought he was silently laughing. We said little for the rest of the day, struggling with our individual thoughts about life and mortality.

When Emin and Edin returned they wanted to check me out to see if I had any wounds. They just couldn't believe that Alen had been shot standing behind me and I didn't so much as have a scratch on my skin or a tear in my clothes. "God protected me," I told them. I repeated it again and again. *"God protected me."* Something awesome had happened. I believed that with all my heart, and I wondered what the outcome would have been if I hadn't picked up the carton of milk when I did. Probably I would have been shot rather than Alen. I couldn't get over it. What had I done to deserve such protection?

Alen survived, although paralyzed and unable to speak. A few days later Smajo visited him and found that Alen could just barely move one hand. Yet, he gradually improved and eventually recovered, becoming the same old Alen we knew and loved.

During one stormy night, Edin and our platoon commander went around the posts to check for casualties. While walking through a small grove, Edin was surprised by the clatter of shells. He found himself in a tight corner with no trenches near by, no shelter, and no way to tell where the next shell would fall. Darkness and trees surrounded him. He hit the ground and remained prostrate until the shelling ceased. Then cautiously, quietly, he inched forward. Suddenly, two late-coming shells hit the spot where he had lain a moment before. He was hit by flying shrapnel, hurt—not killed—but in bad enough shape that he couldn't crawl to cover. A man in a nearby trench heard his moans, crawled out to him, covered him with a blanket, and ran for help. Edin survived, but had to be hospitalized.

We were all badly shaken by his injury. We felt even more vulnerable, as if the invisible shield we'd once enjoyed had been ripped away. We had enjoyed gambling with our buddies, but no longer. We missed their smiles, their jokes, their bravado. As the numbers of our small unit thinned, we all felt a new kind of emptiness. We spoke less, but communicated more.

Near one place where we stayed, a cluster of houses

stood within reach. We thought that searching around them might turn up a chicken, a goose, or even a pig to turn on a spit. So, motivated by a hunger for fresh meat, two of our companions set out to see what they could find. They spent two hours searching the area and found nothing. At noon a gypsy we knew came by. When we told him of our craving, he pointed to the houses and said, "Your lunch is there." We explained that two of our men had searched and found nothing. He smiled mysteriously, walked to the houses, and half an hour later returned with a bag containing a piglet and a rooster. I never eat pork, nor do I care much for fowl, so I didn't join in. However, my buddies enjoyed the feast.

At the time, we were operating in a fairly dangerous position. A river was to our left and in front of us a dirt road rose from a river fjord. We were often under attack from both directions. All around us were piles of earth we used for protection during attacks.

Being so close to the river, the nights were cold, wet, foggy, and miserable. We were always delighted to experience a new dawn. We were camped so close to enemy lines that even a whisper could bring bursts of fire. We tried to breathe noiselessly, and no one dared allow the sound of a snore in the trenches. When we smoked we covered our cigarettes with both hands, bending face down to the ground to keep the red embers hidden from view.

In our six-by-six-foot trench we had a machine gun, several rocket launchers, shells, ammo, and our personal arms. Three or four of us guarded the post. Because it was so crowded, one or two of us would frequently sleep outside the trench behind an earthen ramp. But if we were attacked during the night those of us behind the trench had no place to go. There was nothing to do but just lie on our backs and watch the bullets and flashes tear up the skies.

Beyond the deadly fireworks shone the silent, steady stars so completely disconnected from the man-made hell all around us. The stars seemed to be whispering a statement about life and the wider world in which we lived. *Our* world was made up of dirt and blood, hate and ugliness; the constellations spoke of light and beauty. We were surrounded with chaos; they spoke of order and predictability. I struggled to understand these contradictions.

One morning Emin kept guard while lying in the trench between a gypsy and one of his friends, both in a drunken stupor. The rocket launcher ammo had been placed in a central location. We'd never used it, but if we ever had to Emin and I were the only ones who knew how. The enemy began firing at first light and the firing intensified and continued without ceasing. Emin became so angry that he grabbed the machine gun and started shooting across the river. When a bullet stuck in the chamber, he wanted to remove it. The two drunks next to me ignored him; they never batted an eyelid. So I got up, and together Emin and I fixed the machine gun. All the while the shooting continued. It made me feel uneasy.

"Lie down!" I shouted to Emin, but he kept shooting again and again. I felt my stomach churning, gripped by a premonition. Emin ignored me. He had the machine gun above me, trying to hold it steady against his shoulder. I couldn't stand it any longer, so I grabbed the sleeve of his pullover and jerked him down. He fell, but his hand never let go of the machine gun. Suddenly we felt a violent explosion at the brink of our trench. As Emin fell to his knees a piece of shrapnel shot through his arm and the trench filled with smoke and dirt.

The shooting soon quieted down into sporadic outbursts and I turned my attention to my buddy. Blood covered his right hand. I brushed aside some hot shrapnel and removed his thick army pullover to take care of his wound. As the pullover came from his arm, I saw a hole just below his shoulder. I bandaged his arm the best I could and we climbed out of the trench. I helped him across an open area, through some cornstalks, into the forest, and then sent him off on his own to safety

"What's happening to us, Zeko?" he asked me as we stumbled along together.

"I've no idea, Emin," I told him, "but I guess this is the way it has to be."

I returned to the trench. The two men were wide awake now, their heads throbbing from hangovers. They were keeping guard as best they could. I looked around. Nothing had been demolished, and the trench remained intact. But the machine gun had been torn apart, and the lids of a few ammo cases were missing. Another young soldier checking the trenches spotted the remains of a cumulative rocket that had been fired at us. Those things could destroy a tank! In shock, we pondered what would have happened if it had flown a few feet farther and landed in our trench, exploding all our ammunition. There wouldn't have been enough left of us to bury.

We were a very somber bunch as we quietly considered the recent turn of events. I couldn't help but ask myself *How come you're still alive?*

CHAPTER 6

Escape Into the Unknown

WHILE LIVING in Bosanski Brod, we started to adapt to this kind of life—the hiding, the fighting, the uncertainty—hoping, however, that it was only temporary and that eventually we'd return to our home town. Our old lives seemed a distant memory, yet we longed to return to the calm sameness of the way we used to be. Every time we came back from the front line, we pretended none of what was happening in Bosanski Brod was our business. We were just guests there, having a good time. Sometimes we'd all meet together in the yard of the house where my mother was living. We sat around, eating and making merry to the music of an accordion. When it was time to go back to the front line we could hardly believe it. "Is it possible that two more days have passed?" we asked ourselves. Our laughter and merriment dropped away like old, worn out coats.

Our boys were being killed more frequently than ever. In contrast to the joking and banter we'd enjoyed at home, there was no conversation on the bus going back. Everyone was lost in his own thoughts.

Once, when I caught the flu, I stayed away from the

front line for three days. Though I always dreaded going back, I felt lonesome without my company. Then one morning around 8:00 I noticed a number of soldiers retreating with all their arms and equipment. "What's the matter?" I asked.

"Nobody knows anything, but we're retreating," someone told me.

I returned to my mother's place, had a quick meal, and then, feeling considerably distressed, hopped on a bicycle and rode downtown to check out the situation. I rode around for some time, and everything seemed normal to me. There was nothing out of the ordinary in the way local people acted. I couldn't detect anything unusual. On my way back, I stopped in a store to buy some cigarettes. Then just as I was leaving, I remembered I wanted some chewing gum as well. I turned around, picked up the gum, paid for it and went out the door. As I got on my bike—one foot on the ground, one leg over the seat—I was jarred by a huge detonation at the crossroads right in front of me, only 10 yards away. A black mushroom-shaped cloud of smoke rose up from it, covering everything. My bike was thrown back by the force of the explosion.

A baby cried somewhere on the smoke-covered street. The saleswoman, standing outside the store, started to moan with pain. She'd been hit in her leg by a piece of shrapnel or a piece of stone. As it didn't seem serious, I stepped into the smoke-covered area to see what was happening. I saw two soldiers carrying the unconscious body of a woman from the steps of a shop at the next corner. Her child, no older than 3, called to her. "Mommy, mommy, stand up!" The child was standing next to the body of a large German shepherd and pulling at the woman's hand. A few more people were hurt, but their wounds were lighter, and they could help themselves.

I climbed on my bike and started home. *It's happened again. Others injured, some seriously,* I thought as I pedaled down the street. *But I'm unhurt. Not even a scratch.*

What was the source of my protection? One by one all the nasty accidents I'd seen lately tumbled through my mind. I remembered Alen. I remembered Smajo, now so frightened of going to the front line that he started to stutter every time he had to go. He'd just sit, smoke, and rock forward and backward. He was like that ever since his old friend Alen had been wounded. Then he witnessed the wounding of the commander, Edin. Then there was Emin who was hit in the trench. There were others, too . . . yet every time I could have been hurt, I was somehow spared.

No, I didn't feel charmed. I felt puzzled.

Shells whizzed past me as I rode toward home. I wasn't afraid of the whizzing ones as I knew they were flying above me. However, those that fell nearby were silent. Then as I turned into my front yard and rode past the house, an explosion nearly threw me off the bike. There was such a reverberation that the whole house was shaking, and tiles were falling off the roof. I ran into the house, followed by Nedzad, whom I had met a few minutes before. He had started to go downtown, but changed his mind because of the shelling. Had he continued on his way, he would surely have died. A few houses off toward the center, a huge bomb—we called them hogs—had exploded, making such a big crater that an entire house would fit in it.

I started to think what would have happened if Nedzad hadn't changed his mind, or if I'd stayed a bit longer at that crossroads. Something had impressed me to let those two soldiers take care of that wounded woman. Had we done differently, where would we be now? I felt goosebumps, realizing that making a slightly different decision could have been fatal.

After lunch I heard that the retreating army would not return to the front line. That meant that we'd lose Bosanski Brod. That afternoon I found another bicycle and rode around town. Everything was deserted. Hardly any people were around. A few men and women were sitting on their balconies, mostly retired people who had nowhere to go. I saw only a couple of cars driving around, both stacked with personal possessions for flight.

How did this happen? Bosanski Brod was alive with people this morning; now its houses and streets were deserted! I told my mother to get together our documents and the most basic necessities, just in case.

A friend agreed to let me use his car, so I went to get my parents and the rest of the household. One single car, and so many of us! And no place to go to, either. I didn't know anyone who could take us in. Yet I forced myself to put all such thoughts aside. First things first. We'd take care of the rest along the way. I had neither choice or time. I opened the trunk of the car and threw a few necessities in. My parents and friends stood around in a state of shock. "Here! Hold this," I told someone. "You. Put that box in the trunk." I practically had to order everyone to do what was needed, they were so frightened and confused.

"I know this is quite sudden, but we've got to do what we've got to do," I told them. I urged them—almost pulling them into place—to stand in line in the corridor, to get ready to leave all they knew. Above us, jets were rocketing the industrial zone and the oil refinery in our neighborhood. Bombs and rockets hit the ground in rapid succession, followed by showers of shrapnel and earth. We were in the middle of the fireworks. At last there seemed a lull in the bombing and I told them to get into the car. Five of us squeezed in with difficulty; I'd have to come back for the others later. Then as we were finally about to leave, our neighbor Stana peeked above the wall separating the houses.

"Besim," she called to me, "and where will I go? I was left here all alone. Can I join you?"

In a heartbeat I took in her frightened face and made a decision. "We don't know where to go either, but you're coming with us."

We somehow managed to squeeze her and her large trunk into the car and were on our way! There was no other place to go but across the bridge to Croatia. Just across the river Sava was a neighboring town, Slavonski Brod, but we didn't know anybody there. Suddenly Stana said, "I have a cousin there, but I don't remember where she lives. Near a forest."

How was I supposed to find a forest in a town? Stana

couldn't remember her cousin's name or surname, nothing whatsoever. We reached Slavonski Brod and started to cruise around one of its quarters. I didn't know the town, but I just kept driving, not stopping anywhere. As we passed the town center, Stana spotted a shop she vaguely remembered. She knew one had to go past that shop to get to her cousin, but she didn't know in which direction. We continued to drive slowly, and Stana recognized a few more details. Still she couldn't give me any specific directions. At every street or cross street I had to make a decision to go right or left or straight ahead. Somehow I managed to make the right decision every time. Suddenly tears filled Stana's eyes.

"There it is, dear Besim, there it is! That's the house!"

I slammed on the brakes and pulled up in front of the yard. Jumping from the car, I ran to the house and rang the doorbell. There was no response. I rang it again, then banged on the garage door. Eventually a confused gray-haired man opened the door. His wife stood inches behind him. I didn't have much time for explaining as there were six of us here and six more helpless people we'd left behind.

"Sir," I said, "I don't know you, but this is an emergency. Stana brought us here to your home. I have nowhere to take these people. Could we stay at your place?"

He just stood there, speechless and scared. Why didn't he say something? Didn't he know about people struck by war?

"Only, please, sir . . ." he said, pointing at the rifle in my hand, and the bombs hanging from my belt. Poor man.

I hadn't thought about the picture I made as I stood before him. As he recovered from the shock, he took us all in, helping us to bring in our luggage, too. His son joined us to help and his wife quickly made some tea and offered cookies to us. We filled the room. After a few minutes' recovery, I told Mr. Dimitrije that I had to go back for another group that was expecting me. I took my rifle and hurried away.

By now some of the streets of Bosanski Brod were impassable, blocked by heaps of rubble from buildings that had been hit and destroyed. I fetched my friend's family, and the seven of us crowded into the car, heading out of this town and out of Bosnia for good.

It was already dark and the bombing continued relentlessly. Planes were still circling above, releasing their lethal cargo. Then it started to rain. Every reflex alert, I jerked the steering wheel this way and that to avoid bricks scattered over the streets. Again I was on the way to the long bridge I'd crossed earlier that day. At the very beginning of the bridge, I saw a sight I'll never forget. I saw a man and a woman with two children and carrying two plastic bags, leaving the town on foot, in heavy rain at night. A long steel bridge stretched in front of them. It already resisted numerous shellings and bombings, so strong and reliable it was. But it had to be crossed by car or on foot. And these two people, each of them carefully carrying a child in one arm and a few bare necessities in the other, were fighting to survive, fighting to save their lives. Water streamed down the pavement, reflecting the city lights from beyond the river, and occasional rocket fireballs. The couple kept walking, soaked through, never casting a glance behind.

When we in the car reached the middle of the bridge we were surrounded by another outburst of rocketing. River water splashed high into the air on both sides, as rockets rained heavily down. Lightning flashes illuminated it all, and in the car mirror I saw scared faces behind me. Clutching the steering wheel, I drove on without stopping, hoping that we wouldn't be hit.

Along the wet streets of Slavonski Brod we saw numerous shoes scattered around, both children's and adults'. Strange. At least this town wasn't being bombed. We reached the house with no further disturbances. Now we were really quite a crowd. The 12 of us and the four of them. But our hosts took us all in, and gladly, too.

While still in Bosnia, I'd learned that my sister was in some kind of castle in Croatia, in the city of Marusevac. I tried to think of ways to meet her and then to go on across the border, just about anywhere. For how could I make a living in Croatia? What could I do?

During the following month, I managed to return the military equipment I'd been issued, staying out of the MP's way. Day and night I pondered ways to relieve our hosts of the dozen of us, but I had no idea where to go. All I knew was that I'd had enough of warfare, especially where I didn't belong. It made perfect sense to me to stay and fight for my home town, but why in the world would I go to fight somewhere in Central Bosnia? For whom?

The bridge was demolished the night we crossed and all contact with Bosnia was cut off. Unfortunately, my brigade was left behind, far behind the enemy lines. Three days later they were rescued in a way that was a disgrace. Everyone in the brigade was mad because of that, since it was not the first time that we were made fools of, unnecessarily left surrounded by the enemy. All sense of fighting the war was lost then. We were nothing but figures on a piece of paper, moved about at the whim of commanders. Perhaps a man, a human life, matters; perhaps it doesn't. That's how our brigade fell apart. Any man who wanted to continue fighting could join another military unit. Those who didn't want to, had to make it their own way.

CHAPTER 7

The True Sign

I PACKED THE few things I had, everything fitting in one small sports bag, said goodbye to my family, and started on my way to look for a better way of life than living with strangers. Quite a few guys from the brigade had already managed to pull some strings and left the former Yugoslavia. I didn't have much money, but I had enough to buy a railway ticket to Zagreb. I knew from previous experience that I wouldn't have much chance to hitch a ride in the army trousers and combat boots I was wearing. On my way, I was on a constant lookout for MP's. It was Sunday, and there wasn't much traffic. When I reached Varazdin, I discovered there were no connections to Marusevec, my destination.

With only a handful of change in my pocket, I walked through the town, wondering what to do next. It was the first time in my life that I felt like a homeless person or vagabond. I didn't know how such people made their living, but I had to find out by the end of the day.

The sun was setting and I had nowhere to go. Back at the bus station, I walked around, hoping something might happen. I went to a café and leaned on the bar. A man next to me, obviously a little drunk, was feeding coins into a gambling machine. I ordered a beer, deciding to sip on it for as long as possible, and started to observe people around me. There was a lot of talk, laughter, and jostling. Some of the people were younger than I was. Nursing the beer, I waited for something to happen that might give me a chance of any kind. I spoke to the man at the gambling machine as I watched him insert one coin after another. After a while I gave him a few tips since I occasionally played the machines before the war.

Eventually I was introduced to a young man, obviously a regular patron. By now I was getting familiar with the place and could already tell the regular customers from the onetimers. The young man promised to help me, but he couldn't do so before 10:30 that night. He told me that he had to go somewhere, but he'd be back. I spent the whole evening at the café, hoping this guy wouldn't let me down. He'd given me his word of honor so I expected him to return. Besides, I reasoned, even if he did let me down, I could sleep just about anywhere. I'd gotten used to sleeping in the fields during my war days.

However, I was doing more than waiting on a new acquaintance. I was doing my best to protect the gambling man and his totally drunk friend who sat at the same table. They were in danger of being robbed by the surly waiter as well as a few more patrons. These two men had just returned from Iraq where they'd worked for half a dozen years. Now they were back home, visiting their relatives, completely unaware there was a war in the region. They had large bags filled with cigarettes and whiskey. They also had quite a bit of money which they kept pushing into my hands, trusting that it was safer in my hands than theirs. Each time they did so I pushed it back to them—thick bundles of Deutschmarks and U.S. dollars—warning them not to take the money out of their wallets unnecessarily. "You're a good fella," they kept saying. "You're taking care of us. Have another drink." About 10:00 p.m. a taxi came to take them to a hotel.

Eventually the young man I waited for reappeared. First we tried to get into a disco free of charge. After that failed he took me to a rented apartment where he was staying, to spend the night. In the morning I continued on my way to Marusevec. I hitchhiked a part of my way there, walked the rest of the way, and finally reached the castle where my sister was living. And it was a proper castle indeed! My sister had rightfully called it so. High turrets reached way above the treetops. *Oh, sister of mine,* I thought to myself, *what in the world are you doing here? Are there still dukes and counts in the world?* I stood in front of the imposing building and stared at its huge, black wooden door. Presently I found out that there were no dukes around that place; it was a school.

"I'm looking for my sister; her name is Suda," I told someone at the door.

"Oh, yes. I'll go get her."

I waited at the front door, excited to be reunited with her, but at the same time I felt troubled. I still had no idea where to go, not even which country to go to.

It was a relief when she arrived. I hadn't seen her in a long time. We had lunch with local students, and I was introduced to one of them, a man named Marijan. He encouraged me, saying that everything would be OK, if only I put off making any decisions for a short while. He told me I should stay there a while and get my bearings. Just take my time and wait to see what happened. Suada warned me that none of the students there smoked. I liked that, since for the last several months I hadn't enjoyed the cigarettes I'd been smoking. Being at the school in a non-smoking environment was how I broke the habit after smoking for half a dozen years.

That night I slept at Marijan's place, and the next day I tried to solve my problem. I was assisted by Tihomir, one of the school's lecturers. We decided that my first step was to obtain a release from military conscription so that I could at least travel freely across Croatia. After that, it would be easier for me to figure out what I should do next. So I went to Zagreb with my sister. There we talked to a Mr. Vukmanic. He'd been recommended as someone who could provide temporary lodging for me in his small house until I obtained the documents I needed.

We banged on his door and rang the doorbell for quite a long time, but nobody came. We'd almost given up when a neighbor across the street told us to keep on trying. Eventually, an elderly gentleman with kind blue eyes opened the door. He was chewing something, and mumbled so we could hardly understand what he was saying.

"Who are you? Are you from the power company?" he

THE TRUE SIGN

asked, squinting at us.

"No, we're not from the power company," we replied. We had to speak up for him to understand. "No, we're not from the waterworks, either. We're from Marusevec, you know, and we were told there that you might help."

He explained that his hearing wasn't very good, so after this shouting contest at his doorstep he invited us in. When we explained who we were and what we wanted, he gladly let me stay at his place.

My sister returned to Marusevec the same day, leaving me with my new friend. It seemed a strange situation. The clothes I was wearing were all the property I owned. Suada provided me with trousers, Marijan gave me a pair of shoes, and I had an old jacket that I'd found one cold day back in Derventa, in somebody's deserted apartment.

My landlord's first name was Ivan. He called me Stef because he liked that name. He kept telling me stories about his sons and their colleagues, who were apparently excellent musicians. I became used to talking loud. He played music from the tapes and hummed most of the time. I knew it would take at least eight days for me to collect all the necessary documents, and I stayed at Ivan's place during that time. He offered me books from his collection, so I spent my evenings in solitude, reading and thinking. Almost every day I made my rounds of offices in Zagreb, spending hours waiting in lines for a stamp or a signature. Moreover, offices I needed were scattered all across the city. Thus I spent half the day in the city, and the other half with Ivan in his house.

The whole time I was there he kept urging me to finish my obligations so I could go to church with him. He wasn't aware that I didn't really feel like going to church; that, in fact, I'd never been to a service before and didn't find the thought of going very attractive. But as he kept humming to himself I realized that the idea of my going to church with him made him so happy that he seemed to think we were halfway there already. I tried everything to avoid going, but finally concluded that I couldn't be that ungrateful to my benefactor who was so eager to take me to church. In the meantime, I helped with housework, dusting his apartment, cleaning the bathroom, helping with whatever he was doing.

Early Saturday morning he awoke me and called me to join him for his customary Saturday breakfast. This morning he was dressed up. I grumbled in protest, but he didn't notice. So we left together. I was going to church!

This was my first attendance at public worship, quite different from praying in a mosque. As long as I was there, I decided I'd be extra observant. Ivan left me in the company of the young men and he joined his cronies. He'd introduced me as coming from Marusevec instead of from the front line, and those guys must have been very familiar with it for they asked me a lot of questions about local news and people who lived there. Unfortunately, I'd had only a brief tour of the place where my sister lived, and I couldn't give them much information. I could just describe what I'd seen and the few people I'd met. It wasn't much.

The whole experience turned out to be quite interesting to me. We sang a few hymns, listened to an interesting talk, and gave a small contribution in money. As a part of so-called Saturday school we had a chance to talk about our own experiences, and I found that particularly interesting. Moreover, as speakers and singers took turns, I was glad to see entire rows of young women sitting in front of me. All of them were nicely dressed. I was sitting on the end of the last row, and to get to their row they had to pass by me as if on a catwalk. I leaned back comfortably and started to enjoy myself.

This public worship consisted mostly of listening, though everyone knelt for prayer once or twice. When worship finished, people got up in an orderly manner to leave the building. I watched as row after row they stood and walked out. It took only a moment for me to realize that one was supposed to remain seated until one's own turn to go out came. Thus I could take a good look at every person as they passed me. As I said, one row was almost all young women. I enjoyed watching them as they stood up, readjusted their clothes, and began to walk out. One of them, wearing spectacles and with a purse hanging from her shoulder, gazed steadily in front of her as she marched past me. I couldn't tell why, but I observed her with a special interest, noticing each detail on her face and body. I felt a little embarrassed for doing so, but I couldn't take my eyes off her until she was gone. *What's the matter with me?* I wondered. I'd never looked at anybody else quite the same way.

At last our turn came to leave the room. Ivan quickly found me outside the building and said that his son and daughter-in-law had invited us for lunch. All those people were so hospitable and kind that it seemed slightly unreal. Perhaps being in the war for so long I'd forgotten what normal life was like. I didn't say much at lunch, as I wasn't familiar with their interests. I uttered only a few words about myself and my sister. In the evening we went back to church again. That didn't surprise me at all for, if they have time, Muslims sometimes go to the mosque as many as five times a day to attend services.

This time I sat next to Ivan. He was a joyful man. He never stopped smiling. We joined in singing some lovely, melodious songs, but most of the time we listened to the speakers. After each song and speech, Ivan almost jumped from his chair with enthusiasm, inaudibly clapping his hands and smiling.

"Stef, this is a beautiful song!" he would say. "Listen how lovely they're singing!"

I'd never met such an enthusiastic man in my entire life. He seemed to be finding his inspiration and will to live in those songs. He kept telling me about Jesus Christ and salvation. I had no idea what we were supposed to be saved from, yet each of his stories contained a certain logic, and it was incredible how all those stories could be combined with each other. When we returned home, he continued telling me about the goodness of Jesus. I couldn't understand everything he said, but the kind old man appeared to be telling me something very important, revealing a secret he had found. I found it pleasant to talk with him, as if I was on vacation somewhere in the country, far from the fast-paced life, far from the war. There were just the two of us. In the evening I praised my own God, Allah, for sending me to stay among such good people.

Early the next morning Ivan's daughter-in-law, Brankica, brought some food. Ivan told me she did that each Sunday. I asked her to ask the boys from church if they would lend me some clothes so I could wash the only garments I had—those I was wearing. She left, and I pondered what to do after I was released from the military conscription. The first thing to do, I thought, was to go to some cafés in the city and look for some people I'd heard were in Zagreb. I was eager to get on with my life.

Later that day, to my great surprise, Brankica brought me a bag full of clothes. There was a pair of slippers with some money tucked inside, a few pairs of socks, some underwear, a pullover, and a black sports jacket. All this was a present from those boys I'd met at church. I was overwhelmed with such kindness. *What kind of people were they?* I wondered. *What urged them to be so sympathetic?*

That evening I searched the city hoping to find somebody familiar from my home town, Derventa, who could eventually help me to find a new course in life. I went from café to café to café, and saw quite a few well-known faces, but there was a hollowness to it all that I couldn't describe. I wandered from place to place, and those people veiled in cigarette smoke, in dim enclosed spaces, seemed to be waiting for their lives to end. It was as if they were on some desperate list of the condemned. They wouldn't move anywhere; they felt contented where they were. They had company of similar souls, and they belonged together. They were satisfied with their lot in life and didn't need anything to happen.

Their lives were miserable, but no one had the guts to change anything about it. They breathed, talked, ate, and drank because they were alive. But they had no purpose. If any money found its way to them, it was welcome, and that was all there was to it. I didn't care much about that kind of life. After spending all that time on the front line, I expected things to change. I strongly disliked such a monotonous way of living. Life had to be better than that.

The next day I thanked Ivan for his hospitality and left the city. I don't know what he thought. I was not yet fully aware that he was an important link in the change I was going through. When I thought of my former life and the kind of life my former friends were living in Zagreb and compared it with the confident, lively, more interesting way of living I'd witnessed recently, I was in favor of change. I wasn't attracted at all by the old ways. I wanted to accomplish something new, to reach new goals, to try to control my destiny, rather than be carried away by the current and inert masses of people.

That's why I returned to Marusevec; to rejoin my sister at the college. The staff welcomed me, and I spent six months there on the crossroads of my life, still not knowing which direction to take. Various possibilities kept emerging, but none of them seemed right for me, because there was always some kind of obstacle blocking my way.

As I was searching for the right decision, the dean suggested that I should enroll in the study of theology, and attend lectures at least for as long as I stayed there. I agreed. I just couldn't yet decide the best course of action, and at the school I felt fresh and new. Secluded there from the rest of the world, I wasn't haunted by any force.

Step by step, I grew familiar with Adventist theology, immersing myself into it as deeply as I felt comfortable. Step by step, indeed. As a man of action, I expected that the right moment to move on could occur at any time, but while waiting, I fed upon the Word of Lord. I accepted each new fact I learned because it was in accordance with my own views. I was already familiar with five of the Ten Commandments—the ones concerning the relations between people—so that was nothing new to me. I learned about the remaining five there at the college. That was a complete novelty to me; I'd never heard anything like that before.

While living this peaceful life, I kept pondering about the odd experiences I'd been through, the many times my life had been spared. I told Marijan, the student at whose place I'd stayed during the summer, about them, as well as my dormitory roommates where I lodged during the semester. In reality, my entire experience in Marusevec in 1992 and 1993 didn't help me make up my mind and move me on in the way I expected my life to go. On the contrary, those months of classes and conversations stopped me and pointed me in the opposite direction. In the words of the gospel, this opposite direction could be described as rebirth.

Later on, I realized that it was also a part of the plan God had for me, as well as a miraculous salvation from literal death. From this crossroads of my life, I took a new direction. I would never change again. And I was led further from my former life than I could ever have believed possible.

CHAPTER 8

Stop the Earth, I'm Getting Off

ALTHOUGH I found myself in an entirely new environment, I felt safe and at peace. Everything was new to me. All the campus activities were a novelty, something I'd never had an opportunity to be involved in before.

I applied at the college, and I was invited to attend the lectures there as a guest student. The lectures were held in the old castle, mostly in the Hall of Knights. The castle itself was magnificent, standing tall on an elevated spot, but God's words and teachings were more magnificent by far. Each new truth from the Holy Scripture provided me with new insights and new guidelines for living, new attitudes toward the world and God. Other students were familiar with these things, but it was all brand new to me.

I had some catching up to do as I hadn't attended lectures from the very start, but I worked hard to learn Greek, to study the life of Jesus, to dig into the Old Testament scriptures, commentaries, and critiques. I was interested in everything, wanting to unveil the truth for myself, to seek out the very beginnings of truth. And as I grew familiar with the Bible teachings, I began to find answers to the many questions I'd had about my own life: *Why? How? For what reason?*

There's a proverb that says, "The more you learn, the better you understand that you know nothing." How true that was in my case. As I realized how little I really knew, I developed a burning desire to learn as much as possible and, in fact, to learn to work with my own hands whenever possible. This had a beneficial effect on the practical aspect of my life—I became quite adept at a number of different things.

I began to understand that I was the master of my own happiness. I didn't have to be a part of any trend, a part of any particular crowd. I could choose my own way; make my own decisions. It was a novel idea. It had always been vaguely present, but for some reason I'd never seen it as clearly as I did now.

I shared my dorm room with two roommates, Faraga and Mladen. We were all freshmen. Life with them was dynamic and full of joy. Mladen was extremely cool, while Ervin was a second Einstein, so to speak. I could really relax in their company, forget about all my problems, get offbeat, and feel courageous. Later, after I left for Germany, I understood that they took the place of my former friends in Derventa. They helped me understand that the Lord is full of love and joy. He is not a Lord who frowns and sulks and offers nothing but hundreds of commands and duties.

Ervin always seemed to have a mission. For example, he organized and led prayer meetings. Mladen would play on a borrowed guitar, keeping up our morale and lifting the general atmosphere. Petar, a Slovene from the room next to ours, often came to visit us. He played the guitar while all of us cracked jokes and generally had a lot of fun. Frequently, as we hung out together, I recalled the months I'd spent on the front line and the frightening and wonderful things that had taken place there. As I spoke about the miracles I'd witnessed, my vision of God's protection over me became clearer and clearer. These guys loved to listen to my stories since it was a real-life experience for them. As for me, again and anew I felt filled with awe for God's presence in my life.

As time passed and I began to assimilate the sum of all those circumstances, I felt something happening inside. God was creating a new man within me. At first I hardly knew how to react. There seemed to be a stranger in my body. Everything around me acquired a new sense of reality. I felt the existence of each separate leaf. Each stone had its weight and shape. Each letter on the page brimmed with reality. Every object in my life had its own peculiar warmth, its own shape and size. I was like a baby, learning about the world all over again. Up until that time events of my life passed through my experience as if they were some kind of movie I watched from afar; something unreal. Suddenly I lived in the *now*. I experienced reality. And by regularly attending the classroom lectures, one revelation after another added to my faith in God.

My sister lived in the neighboring dormitory but we met in the lecture rooms, in the dining room, and on the path between the castle and the dorms. Saturdays, the Sabbath, we spent the whole day together.

I played basketball in a pair of long shorts and an oversized pair of shoes that I got from ADRA (an Adventist charity organization). They didn't have my size. Finally one of the boys gave me his old sweat suit bottoms, a bit too short for me, but much more comfortable than jeans. It didn't matter to me that my clothes were mismatched. As my heart changed I stopped caring about the way I looked. I was just happy. I finally felt alive.

And so time passed. My friend Marijan, in his third year of studies, provided me with all the help I needed when I couldn't grasp the meaning of a particular text. He explained to me the relationship between individual texts within the Bible. In a couple months I learned that Jesus was not born of earthly origin; that He came from heaven to live for us and to die to save doomed humanity. It was this—my most valued insight fitting seamlessly into each other insight—that gave a new meaning to my life. It was a fast paced study for me, with countless interesting and unexpected details.

Marijan's parents, who lived in a neighboring village, took a special interest in my sister and me, and when they heard that our parents were in Slavonski Brod, they did everything in their powers to bring them closer to us. At first they invited them to come stay in their own home. Then they started to search for a permanent home for them. All the while, Marijan, my sister, and I prayed to God that our parents might find their special place under the sun, a place to settle down. In a few weeks they moved to Cerje Nebojse, a village not far from Marusevec, settling into a little abandoned two-bedroom house at the very end of the village. We obtained beds and mattresses for them, and they moved in. Immediately they started to cultivate a garden in their backyard. It was easy to see how happy they were to start a new life. Then one afternoon a drunken old woman came to see them, with a very odd remark:

"I came to visit you, and now whatever happens, happens."

My parents offered her what hospitality they could, but they had no idea what she was talking about. Apparently there were rumors in the village that they were some kind of Mujahedins, guerrilla fighters. People in that area hadn't had much experience with war or refugees so I guess they were suspicious. Everybody was afraid of newcomers from Bosnia, and there'd been some talk on TV that real Mujahedins came from the Middle East. People were afraid that something bad might happen if my parents accidentally saw their wives or daughters. Such is the influence of television.

My parents had nothing to do with that kind of people, nor did they dress like the Middle East Muslims. My mother and father were normal, civilized citizens, such as you can find throughout the world. Eventually people realized that these rumors were untrue and they were accepted as members of the community. People helped them as much as they could—bringing them gifts of eggs, cheese, and milk. To return the favor, my parents helped occasionally by working in their neighbors' fields. The owners of the house they lived in were away in Australia, having left 10 years before. They were glad to hear that somebody was taking care of their old home.

Whenever I wanted to enjoy my mother's cooking, I'd rush to their place over the weekend and just have a ball. It was great to have them near, even though they sometimes grumbled about my school. They would have preferred me to be in a state-run college. But in spite of my parents' objections to what I was learning, everything I was taught—the details of the life of Jesus and His mission, and of God in general—added more to my determination to remain in school. In fact, I wanted all the more to stay and feed on the Bible truths I hungered for.

Once as I was returning from the playground to the dormitory, sweaty and short of breath after a baseball game, I spotted a girl who looked very familiar to me. Try as I might, I couldn't remember where I'd met her. But when I got to my room I had a brief vision of seeing her in the church in Zagreb. That was it. Yes, no doubt about it. A month passed; she didn't show up in Marusevec again. I continued with my studies. Now I was learning to type, though I needed a lot of practice.

Then the same girl began showing up at certain lectures. I felt oddly attracted to her. As it happened, in the rooms of the castle where we had classes each door opened into another room. Room 11 was frequently used to study for the lectures or to practice typing. The room next to it, where most lectures were held, was number 12.

Each castle room was unique, its ceilings and walls covered with beautiful detailed artwork. And each room was furnished in a different style. Most of the walls and ceilings were wood paneled, which I especially liked.

I learned that the girl I frequently saw was, in fact, a teacher working in the high school on the campus. In addition, she taught in Varazdin. Whenever she had extra time she attended lectures for her own interest. On one occasion, as she sneaked into the lecture room and stood next to the door, I was passing around some candy to relax students before the exam. Turning to her, I offered her the bag of sweets. "Help yourself," I said, but she declined. Then I said, in a very strong Bosnian accent, "C'mon, pal, have some. Don't be shy." She took one piece and said thanks.

The ice was now broken between us, and my curiosity was finally satisfied as well. Her name was Blanka.

Sometimes we just said "hi" when passing each other; sometimes we'd stop and talk for a little while. Gradually we grew to spend a lot of time together—on our way to the dormitories, at lunch and dinner, in the castle, sometimes at school and on the playground. Blanka proved to be a very interesting person and I enjoyed spending time with her. She was full of life, very ambitious, and capable of doing more than one job at the same time. Plus, she was attending lectures as well. She was brisk and agile; just what I appreciated. After all, I had similar ambitions myself—to learn and understand as much as possible.

As my parents, who now lived quite close, sometimes disapproved of Marusevec, I grew fond of spending my spare time with Blanka. Unfortunately, this caused a certain jealousy in my parents which proved to be a great source of trouble. I was an adult and I could fully understand how my new beliefs and my new friends made them unhappy. It was so different from their own deeply ingrained belief system. But my life had taken a different path. My outlook had changed during the time I spent fighting for freedom, with my life on the line day after day. I'd seen buddies die. I'd struggled with grief and with questions. And now I'd found peace as well as answers to the large questions of life.

But they wouldn't—or couldn't—understand when I talked about my needs and experiences. Their attitude grew steadily worse, until one day they were visited by a stranger. It was obvious that the man was from the Middle East. In fact, he was from Saudi Arabia. He'd heard through the grapevine that my sister and I had strayed from our upbringing, that we'd abandoned our parents, that we were a disgrace to the family, and so forth. He approached my parents under the guise of bringing them some charity help, but before long he confided to my father his sympathy for his wayward children, and offered some solutions. Thus my father sent a message that he was coming to the school to visit, and arrived accompanied by that man.

My sister and I joined my father and the stranger in the old red Mercedes he was driving and we started toward my parents' house. We hadn't gone very far when he stopped the car in a grove along the way and gave us a piece of his mind. He tried to intimidate us, telling us that our presence in that Christian school was a crying shame, that he had everything we needed to get us out of there. He'd send us and our parents to Saudi Emirates. There we would attend a decent school, or, if we preferred, we could get a nice job. We would be nicely taken care of, he said.

He talked fast in a loud, angry voice. He was very pushy. I could see that my father was really angry after everything the man had told him. My sister and I just looked at each other.

"Thanks for letting us know about that," I said when he finally wound down. "We'll let you know what we decided by 9:00 in the morning."

He drove us back to the campus, and he and my father left. My sister and I talked for a long time. We respected our parents. We realized that they were hurt and probably could not understand why we were taking a different path. But we determined we would not go anywhere. We were staying here. If our parents felt they'd be better off without us, they could go and we wouldn't try to keep them here.

The next day I visited my parents and explained that we wouldn't be as free in Sandia Emirates. Customs were different there, I reminded them. We'd be strangers in a foreign land. My parents abandoned that plan but on one later occasion, as I was discussing belief in God with my father, he confessed that he'd had a rifle in the car trunk that day. The man had urged him to kill us if we disobeyed our parents and refused to leave Marusevec.

I explained to my father that God is love, that He is not a judge who can hardly wait for us to make a mistake so He can condemn us. To my shocked horror, my father replied that he should have killed us when he still had an opportunity. He wouldn't speak about it again, though my mother told me a few more details about what had happened.

I was at a crossroads in my life. Either way would require some painful sacrifice. Either I had to return to my parents because of some obscure idea of shame, or I must choose what I felt through my experience to be the truth and reality of life. Both sides held a certain logic to me, and I felt suspended between them. On the other hand, I couldn't understand why some people who had learned about our loving, living God and His son, Jesus, from the Holy Scripture still felt jealousy or envy. I couldn't understand why people who knew these things didn't live according to what they were preaching. These same people were telling Blanka that perhaps she shouldn't spend so much time with me, that nobody *really* knew me. I understood when other girls said that. I knew how girls could be. But I couldn't understand why the rest of them were suspicious of me. It hurt.

I'd spent almost an entire academic year in their company. I'd sat by them in classrooms and eaten with them in the dining hall. I'd played basketball and baseball. I'd laughed at their jokes and they'd laughed at mine. And the love of the God they knew and served had touched my heart and soul. Hadn't they learned yet that I didn't present any danger to them?

Only my roommates understood my heart. That's not quite true. Blanka—who'd only recently found out that I was different from other students, being a Muslim—understood me too.

All of these social problems and difficulties almost made me lose my spirit, almost made me go away, run away from everything. I wished people wouldn't bother with my life, but that obviously couldn't work the way I wanted. I wished I could go where there were no people, but I was a human being, and needed company. Once you escape death and take shelter at some safe place, other problems appear. What seemed so lovely one moment turned into hostility a moment later. Who would rescue me from my mortal life? Life has so many ups and downs. That's why I believed that everything in life was a vanity and a vexation of body and spirit.

Then I experienced something important and powerful. Mladen and I were in charge of delivering and collecting the laundry. We did this once a week, usually after our lectures. One day as I was carrying a basket of laundry behind the girls' dormitory, I met Ljubica, a short thin woman who worked in the laundry room. She was a spirited person with a high-pitched voice, and whenever she had a chance she loved talking about her daughter. Young people generally didn't think her to be very serious. But that day she greeted me cheerfully, and when I was about to continue on my way she took my hand and suggested that I sit on a stair.

She sat down next to me. "Tell me," she said in a surprisingly low and quiet voice, "what brought you to church?"

It was the first time that anyone asked me that question. I was quite taken aback.

"What do you mean?" I replied. Recently I'd gone

about in a state of confusion because of all my worries. It hurt to go against my parents. It broke my heart. And my mind was burdened by the misunderstanding of others who claimed to know and love God but whose suspicions were driving me away.

She leaned closer to me. "Church is a healing house," she said. "This is where you prepare and heal yourself for the heaven. Don't look at people. Look at Christ."

She stood up and left. I remained seated, wondering just what was wrong with her. Why had she said that? Suddenly she returned, said a few more words, then left again.

I stared at my empty laundry basket, wondering how to get a relief from the burden in my soul. I wished I'd never even heard of Christ. I wished I'd never met all those people. As I stared, the basket blurred through the tears in my eyes. In that moment something snapped inside me. I'd passed the crossroads, and since that evening, my only goal was to find Christ for myself.

I went to my room, lay down, put my hands over my eyes, and started to seek Him.

CHAPTER 9

Back to Life

I WANTED TO discover Christ in person, for myself, so I found an illustrated Bible and began reading it from cover to cover. When I told Marijan what I planned to do, he told me that I should pray before opening the pages, asking God to bless me and give me understanding. So I did. I bowed my head and prayed as I opened its pages, reading every night before going to sleep. I was determined to have a complete understanding of Jesus and to learn what Christ meant to me personally. God seemed to shelter me as I read for I wasn't distracted by anything—not my roommates' loud singing or talking, nor the comings and goings of other students. Alone with my Bible, I seemed to be in my own world, my mind drifting through my past, as I searched to understand how God had guarded and led me throughout my whole life.

Each morning when I awoke, even before opening my eyes, my mind turned to what I was learning about Jesus. I was fascinated by His desires and goals for the people He touched when He lived on earth. That was important to me and I felt that I grew closer to Him as I read the Gospel stories. But even more important, I wanted to know what Christ planned for my life. Today. What relevance did the Creator of the world have for me in my small town in Croatia?

And so page after page, I read. From Genesis to Judges, through the psalms and proverbs, from the major and minor prophets to the beautiful story of Christ's birth, life, and death, then stories from the early Christian church, and finally the Revelation of Jesus Christ—I read the entire Bible. And inasmuch as I could understand it at the time, Christ's mission was revealed to me. It was enough for me to know that I must continue the way I had chosen. I had little doubt. There was no need for me to wrestle it through, or to spend days thinking it over. I decided to follow Jesus.

The academic year was finished. I stayed on the campus, along with Marijan, to work for my tuition. Blanka left for Germany, and with her away I realized how attached I'd become to her. As Marijan's girlfriend went home over the summer to visit her family, we were both separated from our sweethearts. He and I were the only workers on campus.

About that same time, my mother and father had to move to a different empty house, in another village. Their neighbors cried when they left, they were so sorry to see them go. They did everything they could to make the move easier for my parents.

I lost 30 pounds that summer, and looked like an inmate of a concentration camp. My ribs stuck out so much that you could count them. Perhaps it was a delayed effect of the war and poor food. Maybe missing both Blanka and my folks made me lose my appetite too; maybe I was working too hard and eating too little. Or maybe it was a combination of things and my body just gave up for a while. I don't know, but eventually I started to recover.

Summer drew to a close and a new academic year started. As I'd missed the first trimester, I began it now with another group of students. As the school year started I decided to thoroughly study the basic truths of the Bible and asked one of the professors to tutor me privately. He agreed, but he was so busy that he hardly ever found time to work with me. Another one agreed too, but he had so many obligations that he couldn't spend more than 10 to 15 minutes a week answering my questions. However, I did get answers to some of my questions about God. Twice I went to Zagreb to talk with professor Kuburic who frequently came to Marusevec as a lecturer. On one occasion I asked if I could talk with him, and he organized a hiking trip to Sljeme, a mountain near Zagreb, for the young people from the campus. We spent a whole day in the mountains and I talked with him about everything that bothered me and everything I couldn't understand.

My questions didn't shock him. He never made me feel ashamed or embarrassed for asking. He is a wonderful man and he helped me a lot. And so I read my Bible, I studied. I asked questions. I listened and prayed. And at last, like pieces of a jigsaw puzzle, I began to put together the picture of God. And suddenly my future appeared brighter.

Finally, I understood! It was as if my faith in God had been floating in midair. I believed, but what did I believe? Whom did I believe in? I didn't know God. I had no concept of the actual war between evil and good that impacted every day of our lives. But now I began to know God! Now I knew why one had to live in this sinful world. I knew where sin and evil came from. I began to comprehend why beauty, like new life, persisted despite ugliness, anger, and despair. I now knew that God had been near me even when I thought there was no God at all. I also learned what He is like. With awe, I realized who had called me by name and saved me from the sniper shot. And I understood the deeper meaning in the story of Jesus' life and death for sinners. The message was clear: God loves *me*. He acts in my behalf, for He is a living God.

I had frequently felt His presence, but at the time it seemed as though I'd only imagined such a thing. Now I read "For God so loved the world that he gave his one and only Son, that whoever believes in him shall not perish but have eternal life" (John 3:16). I was no longer afraid of God. Before I'd imagined God as sort of floating above me, frowning, waiting for me to make a wrong move so He could rebuke me and punish me. Now I knew why I'd escaped death time and time again. I saw His hand and grace in all the miracles that had occurred around me. I was afraid no longer, for I loved Him now. I wanted to meet Him, to spend time with Him.

In order to see Him with my own eyes, I'd have to wait for His coming—hopefully soon—but in the meanwhile I would live happily and gratefully. Now I knew the meaning of the word Messiah, and who He was. I understood what *Id al-Adha* was. My old world had disintegrated, but

I had a new foundation—the God of heaven. The truth of God's love changes people, and it changed me as well. I wasn't the man I'd been before. I looked at the world through different eyes. I thought different thoughts. I was a new man.

CHAPTER 10

God Leads

THEN CHANGES came. After spending almost a year peacefully in the shelter of Marusevec, I was able to move to Germany. Now I could be near Blanka. Looking back, I feel certain that God gave me that special year in Marusevec where He could shelter me within His shadow until I was reborn and became a new person.

Some time before, when Blanka and I had been traveling by bus together, we became acquainted with the driver, told him about my problems—that I needed work and a permanent place to live—and we exchanged addresses. He found a solution for me. I obtained a visa and went to Germany, to Stuttgart. It was a new world.

When I visited an Adventist church, I met a preacher known by his nickname Bacu. He helped me to complete my study of basic biblical truths. He explained historical events so impressively that he seemed like Moses to me. He was strikingly tall, fun to be around, always in a good mood. Conversations with him reaffirmed my decision to follow Jesus.

I was living with the Jobs family where I helped with housework, mostly cleaning around the house and yard. It was something like my first job. Their daughter Steffi also found me a part time job delivering newspapers. Staying in their guest room, I had plenty to be grateful for. Things started to move, a new life was beginning. Without work and a place to live, perhaps I would have been lost, so now I was grateful for everything I had. Soon I made my covenant with the Lord.

Three churches in Stuttgart provided services in my native language (Croatian), so I felt at home. I also met some of the people—now my brothers in Christ—who used to meet in that church where I had kept my guard duty. It was amazing. We talked about Derventa and the people I'd known a lifetime ago. These conversations were especially valuable to me. I'd lost a number of dear family members and friends, but now in Stuttgart I met several families from my home town! What a change this was, in only two years! After all the things I had been through! I could hardly believe it, but I was happy.

Blanka and I continued to spend as much time as we could together, which brought me much joy. I was in an unfamiliar city, unable to even speak the language properly which was difficult indeed. Still, the love we felt and shared made it much easier for us to overcome the big and small problems we encountered every day. As to the things that brought us joy, being together helped us enjoy them all the more.

In the center of the city lived another of our sisters in Christ—Aunt Ana. We visited her often. We called on her whenever we went to her part of the city because she provided us with a lot of support. She helped us to find work. She translated what we needed translated. She offered us food to eat and and a place to rest. She simply welcomed us and loved us. Her home was a safe, quiet, warm place, where we were understood and accepted. She was like a mother to us.

Then Blanka and I decided to marry. Up until 10 days before the wedding we still didn't have a place where we could live together. We had only one suitcase each, so when we finally found a place to live, moving was a simple affair. We found two mattresses in the street and brought them home by subway. (That was an experience!) Our charity organization, ADRA, provided us with our first furniture—a small table and a chair.

Though we didn't have much money we still wanted to dress up on our wedding day. We wanted a wedding gown for Blanka, then after the ceremony we'd take a ride around the city, and finally go for a pizza, still wearing our wedding garments. We thought that would be fun, because people celebrated in many different ways all over the city. Some of them rented an entire tram car, then partied while riding around all day.

The city center was filled with street musicians, mimes, illusionists, and sketch artists. Everything seemed completely spontaneous, and it was a true pleasure to just walk around town. Like two turtle doves, Blanka and I strolled from one shop window to another. We watched the mimes and musicians performing their acts, and we laughed and hugged each other. We imagined creating our own home, decorating it, living in it, and so bearing witness to our belief in the true God.

It was in fact so nice, that sometimes I still wish I could go back to that way of life. We didn't feel that we lacked anything. As a young couple, we soon made many friends, and we spread the word of God among them. Our commitment to God must have been obvious, for people often commented on it—that we were unlike other people, that we were somehow different, special—but we couldn't feel it ourselves. We didn't intentionally act or live in a way that would set us apart. Having others tell us that we were different was the first time I actually experienced that when God changes you things are different both inside and out! He did that for me, and I realized anew how wonderful and great He is.

Our apartment was quite roomy. It was similar to a gallery with lots of small windows on one side, overlooking the gate leading into our yard, and a pond just across from our front door. A small creek ran into this pond, gurgling softly day and night. Each morning sparrows gathered there, dived into the water and chirped brightly. They were as punctual as the clock, and awoke us at the same time each morning.

Living together was a blessing, a novelty for both of us. We could hardly have imagined how happy it made us. Marriage was surely invented by God's great wisdom, as it brought such joy and pleasure every time you realized that you belonged to somebody. Blanka and I fulfilled each other. If there was something one didn't know, the other one supplied the answer. When one was tired, the other one was strong—just like one being.

I grew all the more convinced that God had prolonged my life. Every day He revealed His glory to me, enabling me to see how wonderful life is, and how wonderful are His plans for His children on earth. Never could I have imagined my life as it turned out to be—through choosing my life companion, giving us a happy time, and experiencing the beauty that learning the truth about God brings. One thing that I now knew for certain: my God never leaves me alone. He helps me to make the best of each decision I had ever made, so I can celebrate Him, the Creator of heaven and earth, the Saviour of the whole world, and my personal Saviour. He rescued me from both the battlefield and the abyss of sin. He set me back on my feet and revealed to me the paths of a better life.

Blanka and I didn't like to be separated so I accompanied her when she went to work. As I helped with her duties we finished in half her usual time. Most of these jobs consisted of housework round people's homes, cleaning and tidying up. For a while, I washed cars by hand at an open used car fair. And then our faith was tested in an unexpected way. Blanka became ill and our doctor told us that she was pregnant, but that it was an extrauterine pregnancy. She suffered dreadful pains. The doctor recommended that the pregnancy should be surgically interrupted, and as soon as possible, too. As there was a very small statistical possibility that our baby could be born, we asked the doctor if we could wait a little bit longer, hoping for a miracle. He agreed, but warned us that even if the birth turned out successfully, the baby might have brain damage and be retarded.

And so we waited. Blanka endured several more days of pain and we did a lot of praying together for God's grace. She was at home now, though I continued to go to work. A difficult weekend finally came to an end and the checkup on Monday showed good signs of recovery. The baby's progress was carefully monitored throughout the pregnancy to spot any abnormalities in development.

It was a valuable confirmation that God hears and answers prayer, for the doctor, as well as for us. One lesson after another, we learned together that God doesn't leave us, that He's always with us, whatever we do, wherever we go, whatever decision we make. And indeed, this experience reconfirmed for us that God never forgets us. It may only appear to us that our course of life should be different, but no matter what happens, God is in control and will bring good out of the worst circumstances.

All during this time I was trying to find a steady job, for we needed every penny. We asked around in churches. We asked our Christian brothers who had small businesses if anyone needed an extra helper, a man ready to do any kind of work whatsoever. Yet, there didn't seem to be any work available. They promised to call me if they needed an extra pair of hands, but the call never came. As we'd finished with all the part-time jobs we'd previously had and were unable to find any new work, we were suddenly jobless. Well, Blanka couldn't work anymore anyway, so it was up to me. That was fine—if only I could find work!

Day after day we scoured through newspaper advertisements. Nothing. On the last day of the last work I had we knelt and prayed and gave our problems to God. We felt confident that He would take care of us for He promised "So do not worry, saying, 'What shall we eat?' or 'What shall we drink?' or 'What shall we wear?' For . . . your heavenly Father knows that you need them. But seek first his kingdom and his righteousness, and all these things will be given to you as well. Therefore do not worry about tomorrow, for tomorrow will worry about itself. Each day has enough trouble of its own" (Matt. 6:31-34).

The next day Blanka and I took a walk in a park, looking for any job advertisements we might see. We paused and prayed whenever we felt the need to. By evening we'd begun to wonder what we'd do now, but as usual, we waited for God to provide for us. At 9:00 that night the phone rang. Blanka answered. A man I didn't know was calling. He asked for me.

"You're out of work?" he asked me.

"Yes I am," I said.

"Would you like a job?"

"Oh yes! Just tell me what to do and where to go."

The address was in a part of the city completely unknown to me. I'd never seen that man, nor had he seen me, but I trusted I'd find him with no problems. In the morning I boarded an overcrowded tram and went to Felbach. When I got off the tram I found myself among a large crowd of people coming and going in all directions. I just stood there and watched for a few moments, then noticed a young man who was obviously on the lookout for somebody, too. I approached him and we recognized each other by the way we smiled, and introduced ourselves. I got into his car and he gave me a ride to work. I was hired by a store that sold all kinds of chocolates and sweets on one hand, and wine and spirits on the other. It had a wine cellar underneath.

My German was very poor, to say the least, but I met my employer and started to work. As it happened, it was raining so hard that I was soaked through in minutes. A new shipment of drink had just arrived—hundreds of cases of beer and wine. It was just the two of us and besides unloading the crates, we also had to serve the numerous customers. We really hustled! I got a pay raise on the very first day of work, which was quite unusual, as other employees had gotten their raises only after a long trial period. The problem of supporting our family was solved, at least for the time being. We were additionally encouraged by that experience, although our future was still unclear.

During the time I held this job, I rode the tram to work, about an hour in each direction. That gave me plenty of time to read the Bible. Blanka and I became acquainted with all the people who lived around us, and soon acquired quite a few friends. This circle expanded all the time. She wasn't allowed to do any work, so we rented an old piano so she could practice and keep up with her music. She also started to give piano lessons to several students. That also gave her an opportunity to share her faith. During her pregnancy, and after our son was born, she continually had students she could instruct regarding their relationship with God. We made some lasting friendships that are still very valuable to us. For example, we met Regina and Ralf, who later became our best friends. We met them when we moved to a new two-bedroom apartment, closer to where I worked.

Unfortunately, however, our moving there was bad timing. We'd planned to be in the larger apartment before the baby was born, but things didn't happen the way we planned. We'd bought a tiny old car, and were running out of money. One day right at the end of the month, we had just 60 pfenings to our name. I left this money—just enough for two phone calls—in Blanka's purse, and went to work. All our belongings were packed into cardboard boxes and we were ready to move to our new place the following day.

The baby was due in two or three weeks, but he had his own opinion about it, and decided to hurry up. Blanka used the money I'd left with her to call me at work and tell me she was in labor. Then she grabbed her things, got in the car, and drove herself to hospital. I quickly left work to join her.

We'd thought about and planned for this day for so long, and now it was here! Blanka had wanted to listen to Tschaikowsky while giving birth, but this was so sudden that we hadn't managed to get a tape or disc. The hospital nurses thought it was a lovely idea and would have granted it, but we had to give it up because there was no tape. Besides, things were moving pretty fast.

The midwives were so amazed at Blanka that they kept crossing themselves. They'd never seen a pregnant woman drive herself to the hospital, and then give birth only two hours later. And that's how we got Ruben—in the middle of moving between two apartments. Because of all those circumstances, and of our musical request, the nurses remembered us well at that hospital. We paid them a visit a few years later, and they could still remember us and Ruben. Moreover, now they play classical music all over the maternity ward, as they found it had therapeutic effects on pregnant women.

We shared all our joys and sorrows with another couple who were both doctors. The four of us had our faith reconfirmed when God granted new life to both our families. As we prayed together and supported each other, we witnessed a true divine intervention in their lives. A healthy son was born to them three and a half years after our Ruben.

After nearly two years of working in Nellingen, in the Notheiss store, I learned some German. Blanka was doing much better. She even took a class in it. Then I found a job on the other end of Stuttgart, as an electrician in a small private firm. We soon changed our apartment for a three-bedroom one, closer to my work. As usual, wherever we lived we soon made friends with our neighbors.

Ulbach is a little village in the suburbs in a valley between three vineyard hills, which had apparently belonged to Princess Katarina. Promenades and riding tracks that were created during her time were still in use. And it was in that apartment where we witnessed Ruben's first conscious prayer. It happened like this. For two months Blanka and I had been praying to God for an opportunity to buy a new car. (Our old car had to be sold when we moved.) Ruben suddenly joined us, knelt, and started to pray. We were pleased indeed. And then, to our surprise, just as we were saying Amen, we heard his little voice. Fervently he said, "Please God, give us that car already. You see that we need it. We have to drive so we can be good and eat well. Amen!"

We met some refugees from Bosnia, nice people with whom we spent some time and helped each other out for the remainder of our stay in Germany. Most of the people in that village were born there and almost every house had a vineyard or a garden. Early each morning Blanka went out shopping.

In the front yards of each house stood tables covered with all kinds of garden products—raspberries, apples, strawberries, whatever was in season. A small tin box sat on the table. You took whatever fruit or vegetables you wanted, paid for it, took your change from the tin box, and you had some fresh produce to go with your cereal for breakfast.

Soon after Ruben's prayer we saw an advertisement for a used car. We called early in the morning and arranged to see it in the evening. That was another miracle, since after talking with us, the man refused to negotiate with any other potential buyers throughout the day. Because we'd asked God to help us find a car, we promised

God that as far as possible, we'd use it to help others. We wanted to praise the Lord with good deeds in this way, as well to use the car, for our own good. We were able to buy it with what money we had, and are still driving it. Thank God, it's been remarkably resistant to breakdowns, and we've never had an accident with it, either.

Blanka still had her piano classes, though now she started to teach at her students' homes as well. She also started a youth choir in a German Adventist church. We called it Asante Imana. The church pastor became another good friend of ours. We found much joy and pleasure in that period of our life.

When Blanka began working with young people at Ruit church, we faced a meaningful task with a serious responsibility. The choir members ranged between 14 to 23 years of age. On the one hand, teenagers can embrace a new activity with lots of enthusiasm, but on the other hand they can be easily distracted. We suggested that the choir should expand their activity from mere singing to include a prayer group. With both songs and prayer we hoped to bring joy and encouragement to our neighbors, both at church and in our everyday life.

Initially, of course, we had to devote quite a bit of time to rehearsals, to create some sort of a repertoire. Before long we were nearing the Christmas holidays and decided to make our first public performance in the city of Esslingen. On one of the busy streets we put up a book stand and sang Christmas carols, accompanied by a guitar. That was our first big step, and all the members of our newly-formed choir were delighted.

It was lovely to see their young, glowing faces as they sang from their hearts, their words and expression speaking of their faith in God. We'd frequently heard various singing groups in the church, and sometimes they'd get virtually out of control and start competing with each other. They seemed to have forgotten the true purpose of music—to celebrate God and help others meet Him too. That's exactly what Blanka and I wanted to achieve in our choir. Thank God that our young friends also recognized that and devoted themselves to this important goal.

One day we were invited by pastor Drago Brozovic to visit a seriously ill sister from our church and sing a couple songs to her. Drago told us that she longed to hear our young peoples' choir; that this was, perhaps, her last wish.

This was on a Thursday. The woman lived quite a distance from us, and everybody was either working or at school. Still, Blanka was determined to bring most of the members to her home. All the young people agreed to come and we paid her a visit in the evening.

My wife found it a truly difficult task to sit down at the piano and start playing, as our sister was gravely ill indeed. Still, we sang boldly, with tears in our eyes. As one song followed another, our sister was visibly overjoyed, and we were able to share in her joy. To conclude, she wanted us to sing *Vather Unser* (Our Father), which we gladly did. We could feel a special kind of peace in the air, signifying God's presence. We were all so touched and happy that we could celebrate God in this way, while bringing her encouragement at the same time.

You know, when you do a good deed that blesses someone else, God draws you, too, closer to Him. This experience provided us all with additional energy to work.

In downtown Stuttgart, our youth set up a stand with religious books in various languages. We were allowed to offer people books several times a week, provided that we didn't charge for them. Still, often those who approached the stand or took a book left small amounts of money to be given to charity. Practically everybody could find something that interested them, and in their own native language. There were brochures and booklets in Japanese, Chinese, English, and various African languages.

The choir also sang at the dedication of a man whose life had gone bad. He had taken to drink, lost his friends, and wasted all his money. Desperate, he intended to take his own life. He made a hangman's knot in his own apartment so he could hang himself. It was quite late at night, but he wanted to relieve his soul in some way, so he reached for the phone and punched a number at random. He just wanted to tell someone he was going to kill himself. His call was answered by an Adventist pastor. After a prolonged conversation, the pastor asked if he could come visit him, instructing him not to do anything before he arrived. When they met, the man started telling the pastor about his problems. The pastor took an empty bag and put all those problems into it. Then he tossed this bag up—to God. He showed the man that the problems had disappeared, and there was no more need for him to kill himself. This man, once so desperate, was transformed into another person.

On one occasion our young members joined the congregation in the Day of Open Doors. Some members were doctors by vocation, so the church and its front yard became a clinic for a day. We sent out advertising posters stating that anyone could have their blood pressure measured, heart rate checked, height measured, and a general physical examination. There was a crowd all afternoon, to whom young members of *Asante Imana* presented their own experiences. As a special program a mime show presented human alienation from one another and the individual's need for a true God.

CHAPTER 11

A New Start

MEETING OTHER people, sharing happy and less happy moments was an important part of our lives. By spending time with other young adults from church we sought to fill the emptiness present in every human heart. We met together once a week, especially on Saturday nights. We enjoyed visiting in each other's homes, too. Then there was the extra special day when friends surprised me on my birthday.

First a friend called, asking me to help her fix her washing machine. "It doesn't seem to work well," she told me.

I'm always glad to help my friends, so I picked up my tools, got into my car, and went around to her place. When I asked what was wrong with the machine, she just shrugged. I tinkered with it a bit and was puzzled to find that there was nothing wrong with it. We talked a little and then her husband said, "Come on, don't pull his leg. You know there's nothing wrong with our washing machine."

Well, OK. I didn't know what was going on, but we had some juice and I returned home.

There I found another surprise. I couldn't unlock the door. I rang the bell but there was no answer. I tried to insert the key again, and suddenly the door opened just a crack, but slammed shut a moment later as if someone very strong pushed it from the inside. About that time I began to wonder if I was at my own apartment or not.

Then someone tall opened the door and stepped out of the darkened corridor. This person had a kerchief wrapped around her head and wore heavy makeup. Now I was really confused. I'd left home only a short time before with only Blanka and Ruben in our apartment, so who was this? Those blue eyes, the height, a blond lock of hair—all those details reminded me of my mother. But she'd never make herself up like that, and she certainly wouldn't slam the door in my face. Then that half-female person opened the door slowly, inviting me in. Her voice was shrill and her buttons were practically bursting off her well-swollen shirt above a huge skirt. Both the eyes and the voice seemed vaguely familiar, but they just didn't fit into any ideas of who it could be.

Suddenly, all the lights were switched on and the masked crowd filling the room burst into singing Happy Birthday. I was flabbergasted. I'd never been so surprised in my entire life.

In the half hour I'd been gone my friends had turned the apartment topsy-turvy. They practically broke in, decorated the rooms, brought a cake, blew up balloons, and gave me quite a start. That "female" who opened the door was actually Mark—a good friend and a brother from the city. It was the first time I'd ever shed tears on my birthday, but as I sang with them I cried with happiness. I still

A NEW START

remember all those laughing faces. I don't have a blood brother, but I found in those people my brothers and sisters who shared their joys and their sorrows with me. Jesus said that one who has lost a brother or sister for Him would find hundreds of brothers and sisters. Was that the reason that I'd had only one sister in my youth? That didn't really matter, I was truly happy.

Many of us met together almost every Saturday night. After the church service a few of us young couples made arrangements and we'd all come to one of our homes. It wasn't only couples, of course. Everyone who wanted to join us was welcome. We all cherished each other's company. In our search for new friends, Blanka and I visited a German church in Ruit (a Stuttgart quarter) where our dear friend Drago Brozovic served as a pastor. At our first visit we realized that this congregation was a bit special. They never failed to notice a new face. There was such liveliness in that church that most of the members came up and introduced themselves to us during our very first visit. The atmosphere was great, and everybody felt at ease.

As I've already said, God can use every move we make to celebrate His name, and this one visit evolved into missionary work for us. Although we had attended just to see some of our friends, we managed to meet everyone from the church. And little by little, quietly supported by the pastor and the large youth group, Blanka agreed to lead a large number of young people in celebration of God by song.

I'd never sung publicly in my youth, nor is my voice trained, but despite that, before long my moment to sing arrived. Not that I lacked reasons to sing in praise of God. Oh, no, I had every reason to praise Him. He had protected me at the front line and in street fights. Many times I had to brush hot pieces of shrapnel out of my hair, but none had ever disabled or even hurt me. Several times I'd been rescued from certain death. Finally, I wanted to sing because I had a new life, a family, and many friends who shared my beliefs.

Blanka had comprehensive musical training, so she taught me how to read music and sing. We practiced a number of songs from their choir list and then I could help her by knowing the new songs she brought to the choir. In this way we helped their church to form an active youth choir which sang in several more churches. We were warmly welcomed and that filled us with new strength to make progress and learn new songs. Blanka doesn't put up with superficiality, so we frequently met for practice and rehearsals. We worked hard to follow Blanka's direction and to sing as strong and as professionally as possible.

Even before Ruben learned how to walk, we had him with us at those rehearsals and he became a favorite of the choir. Everyone loved him and petted him, and he started to receive serious musical training as a baby.

We were very busy, too busy. Besides our regular jobs, the youth choir and other church work seemed to take all of our time. We suddenly found ourselves seriously overworked, so we had to find a solution for that. We honestly wanted to work for other people—not only for ourselves—but it came to a place where we had no time left for our

A NEW START

own needs. We were in a routine and didn't know what to do to slow down. Blanka and I were afraid that our family would suffer, as we felt that we were losing control of our own lives. And so as with all our other problems, we turned to prayer.

We knew that we should, by no means, let our marriage come unstable. If that happened, all our eagerness to work for God and all the hours we spent working with young people wouldn't be worth much. We started to pray that God would give us more time for ourselves. We prayed that rather than be overburdened by too much work and too many duties we would find time for each other.

God gave us the thought of taking time each evening for a long walk in the vineyards that grew in the hills above our home. There were so many paths and hills that we never had to take the same route twice. But we still hungered for special time together, and we prayed to the Lord to help us organize our own lives in the most efficient way possible, keeping in mind the needs of our family.

After a few months, something happened that at first seemed more like a curse than a blessing. After a few years of driving my car without any problems, I was stopped by a routine police patrol. They checked the car and my documents, and just as they were about to let me go on they asked for my ID, my driver's license. Bad news! They discovered that I'd already spent three years in Germany, while my driver's license which was issued in Croatia, was valid only for two. We had to obtain German papers and didn't dare to drive until we got them. They were quite costly, however—

totally beyond our means—so we couldn't use our car anymore. We hardly knew what to do next. We really needed the car badly, since the city was five miles away and Blanka's students were scattered around in a circle of about 15 miles. I could ride my bicycle to work (I still had an electrician's job). That wasn't a problem, but there was Blanka's job to think of. In addition there were choir rehearsals, Saturday services, concerts, prayer meetings.... We were forced to let our car sit in front of our apartment building and take the buses and subways and to use our own two feet. It was necessary for us to leave our place 10 to 20 minutes earlier than before to wait for public transportation.

This took more of our time, but then again, we reduced our trips away from home to a bare minimum, so we suddenly had more time for each other. In addition we found that while waiting for our buses and riding them, we had extra time for talking together. We were on time wherever we went; as a rule, even 10 minutes earlier than before. In a few days, we were thanking God for getting us out of the car and making us happier. After living together for years we were getting acquainted again and we liked it! We recognized that being stopped by the police was an act of God and His help, not a curse, so we were grateful. We realized that while things in life don't always work as we plan, God can use circumstances to give us a greater blessing.

Through this experience God taught us three important lessons. First, that it was impossible to sit on two chairs at the same time; second, that everything around us was only temporary, and not always as valuable as we

A NEW START

thought; and third, that the family is Satan's favorite target. But God is willing to help, if needed and wanted. God answered our prayers in a very simple way, and pointed us back to true values.

We were living in Germany as displaced persons, so our stay there was only temporary. Every couple of months we had to apply to extend our permits. Then one day the permits were denied. We receive our notices a few months before our visas expired, so had some time to figure out where to go next. Blanka has relatives in Australia, so we applied for a visa there. Unfortunately, our application wasn't granted. We couldn't understand it, for we met all the conditions for granting a visa. We continued to pray about it and finally decided to abandon that plan. Another interesting destination for us was Norway, but we didn't have any success there, either. Then we tried Austria, with the same result. Finally we realized that all the roads were blocked for us, with the exception of Croatia.

So the decision was made. We'd go back to Croatia.

It was going to be difficult to leave our friends, and we decided to give a parting concert in Ruit. Our youth choir was named *Asante imana*, which translated from a South African dialect, means "Only God be thanked." Blanka and I decided to reach out to our dearly loved friends one more time with that concert. We hoped to somehow bring God's great love closer to them through our message. *Asante imana* was more than a group of singers. We were a praying group, too, and had been blessed with living experiences in our meetings with God.

These answers to prayer were very encouraging to us, so we decided that for our last concert we would more than just sing. We'd also tell some of our personal experiences with God. It was a novel concept for a concert, but when Blanka suggested it, everyone agreed.

I feel obliged to mention at least one of the experiences shared that day. A young woman named Michaela (Michi) and a young man, Florian, (Flo) were driving along Highway A-8, one of the most highly-traveled German highways. They were driving in the fast lane, behind a truck. The truck driver flipped his right blinkers, indicating that he wanted to move into the adjoining slower lane, but he must have misjudged the gap between cars. There wasn't enough room for him to get over and he hit one of the vehicles. Michi and Flo couldn't see what was going on, but they slammed into a car in front of them at full speed. The car on the right which was hit by the truck, lost control and sped left, with dreadful results. The four passengers in that car were killed, in front of our friends' eyes.

What about our friends? The best way to describe it would be to quote the famous passage from Psalm 91:11: "For he shall give his angels charge over thee, to keep thee in all thy ways" (KJV). As our friends described it, they were "reborn." They came out of this accident like those young men out of the fiery furnace, unharmed. How merciful and good God is! Their testimony will surely remain in the hearts of all the people present at our farewell concert.

Blanka and I had become emotionally attached to those people beyond words, and it was truly difficult to say

A NEW START

goodbye. After the concert, the congregation of the Ruit church surprised us with a banquet for all the guests. We'll remember it for as long as we live. It's a wonderful thing when brothers and sisters live together in joyful harmony. Our friends present at the concert who were not Seventh-day Adventists couldn't believe that there was still love among people. Many of them thought about their own lives that night, and I pray that God will bless them all and bring them into His kingdom, so we may some day celebrate His name together.

Three more weeks remained until the end of our stay in Germany, and we still had no idea where to go. Then on a Saturday in July we attended a large Seventh-day Adventist congress in Schleir Halle, the largest hall in the city. It seated 10,000 people. Robert Folkenberg, the president of the General Conference at the time, was coming to speak and we could hardly wait to hear his spiritual message. In addition, Blanka and I wanted to meet him for a very special reason. We'd heard from our brothers from the former Yugoslavia that brother Folkenberg had visited Derventa, my home town, and seen the torn-down church there. On that occasion, he learned that one of the local Muslims found Jesus Christ. He was interested in the story, and wanted to meet me. That's why I was also especially eager to see him at the congress.

Our meeting was arranged, and we were both pleased. He asked me a few questions concerning my conversion and suggested that I should write a book of my life. He said that the life story of a man who had been lost, and then, by God's mercy, was found again would be a blessing to others. I'd never thought about that before.

"What good is it to experience God's personal presence in one's life," he asked me, "and keep quiet about it?"

I couldn't get his words out of my mind. *How could I write a book?* I wondered. *I'm not gifted enough for that.*

My wife encouraged me to start putting the story of my life on paper and we decided to look for a person who could assist me. Unfortunately, nobody could give us that kind of help. After two years of thinking and praying, I decided to write it on my own.

Brother Folkenberg also considered our immediate problem, the fact that we had to leave Germany in a very short while. Indeed, a mere two weeks before the deadline we still didn't know where to go. All doors seemed closed to us. On that special Saturday, 10,000 believers prayed for us, and for days afterward we received dozens of supporting phone calls from our brothers and sisters in all parts of Europe.

Through fervent prayer, Blanka and I decided that our best course of action would be to return to one of the countries we'd come from, Croatia or Bosnia. It was the best decision at the moment. However, it wouldn't be easy. It was very difficult to find work in Croatia, for unemployment was extremely high. But that was just another reason to pray all the more. We knew that if God wanted us to return to Croatia, He would also take care of our bare necessities. That's exactly how it was.

On July 1, 1997, we left Germany and came to Croatia,

A NEW START

where at first we stayed at my wife's parents' place. We were received there very warmly. We took a few days off to rest and recharge our batteries, then started to look for work. Blanka found work immediately as a music teacher in a local high school. I found a job in a couple of days, too. Blanka's father, Milan, had been asked to recommend a reliable, hard-working young man who'd be willing to work for a private entrepreneur. I was the obvious choice, being his son-in-law. At the moment, I was still in Germany, but my future employer, Mr. Ignac, decided not to hire anyone until I returned.

Finding work so quickly was a great miracle for us, and this experience taught us anew that one should always put oneself in God's hands and trust Him unconditionally.

My employer was a stone mason. In addition, his company serviced diamond cutting tools—a very interesting and well-paying work. His plans were to give me a training in his line of work, and later I would perhaps inherit his business. In this job, too, I had plenty of opportunities to tell people about God and my beliefs.

My wife also had numerous spiritual experiences in her work at the high school. One is well worth mentioning. She had a student in the first grade of high school, named Ivana. Toward the end of the academic year, Blanka noticed that something wasn't right about Ivana. She seemed exhausted, and she had severe headaches. Then a while after that Ivana stopped attending classes. My wife learned that the girl had cancer of the lymph system.

Blanka took the news very hard. It was difficult to believe that the life of such a young, talented girl was hanging in the balance. It was during summer holidays, so one day she visited Ivana at her home. Blanka talked to Ivana's parents about changing Ivana's diet to vegetarian, and bought different fruit and vegetable juices for her from Austria. The most important thing, though, was that the next Sabbath in our small church we decided to pray for Ivana's recovery .

Her doctors' predictions weren't at all good, but Ivana, who prayed with us, started to firmly believe that God could heal her. And indeed, after only two radiation sessions, all the tumors disappeared. For all the people who saw Ivana and her parents with their own eyes, that was a living example of God's power to heal. As for our little church, it was a great event brought about by sincere prayer.

As a church, we then understood something else. When the faithful pray together over a problem, they are closer to each other, and there are no conflicts between them. Through such prayer God Himself can be trusted to bring a solution. If you, who are reading this memoir, have any problems in your church—if you don't understand each other—start praying for a common cause, and such problems will vanish. This experience made us stronger, gave us power to go on in both our personal and spiritual lives. I believe that God leads us even when we cannot see the future. For in each situation we found ourselves, we could witness for our faith, draw valuable conclusions, and experience God.

A NEW START

We are still in Croatia now, trying to do everything in our power to spread the glory of God. We haven't settled down or grown tired. It seems that we don't even know how to do that. Each new environment provides a new challenge.

We thank God for our temptations, too. Like all people, we too are embittered by fallacy and injustice. We toil along our narrow path, but we are also happy, for we know Who we belong to, and Who leads us on our way to Heaven. We wouldn't want to let our Saviour down, but do everything in our power to spread the joyful news about Him. That's why we left East Croatia, after spending two years there with well-paying jobs. Instead of staying where we were comfortable, we decided to prepare ourselves for a further step in God's work. I am now studying at Adriatic Union College, and it is our greatest wish to help carry the message which the three angels are spreading around the world. I sincerely hope that the road I've taken thus far can be useful to other people who are in their own way of getting to know Jesus Christ and His missions, and point to the true values in life. Moreover, I wish I could encourage everyone by helping them understand that God acts in behalf of all people. I want them to know that He invites everybody to Him—regardless of one's color, nationality, or social status—for everything is bare and revealed to God. He doesn't recognize the limits that set us apart.

Don't be afraid, for God awakens the best in everyone, even the desire to find out who He is. For me too, it was a great piece of news to learn that I wasn't seeking God, but that all that time when I thought I was alone, He was seeking me! He found me. If anything urges you from within, making you want to learn more about God, listen to your heart. Look for Him in the holy Bible, and ask Him to open your spiritual eyes, so you can see that He is a living God. "Ask and it will be given you; seek and you will find; knock and the door will be opened to you. For everyone who asks receives; he who seeks finds; and to him who knocks, the door will be opened" (Matthew 7:7, 8).